7

CORE SKILLS

Language Arts

ISBN 0-7398-7094-7

© 2003 Harcourt Achieve Inc.

Printed in the United States of America.

5 6 7 8 9 054 09 08 07 06

Steck Vaughn™

A Harcourt Achieve Imprint

www.Steck-Vaughn.com
1-800-531-5015

Contents

Introduction

Core Skills: Language Arts was developed to help your child improve the language skills he or she needs to succeed. The book emphasizes skills in the key areas of

- grammar
- punctuation
- vocabulary
- writing
- research

The more than 100 lessons included in the book provide many opportunities for your child to practice and apply important language and writing skills. These skills will help your child excel in all academic areas, increase his or her scores on standardized tests, and have a greater opportunity for success in his or her career.

About the Book

The book is divided into six units:

- Parts of Speech
- Sentences
- Mechanics
- Vocabulary and Usage
- Writing
- Research Skills

Your child can work through each unit of the book, or you can pinpoint areas that need extra practice.

Lessons have specific instructions and examples and are designed for your child to complete independently. Grammar lessons range from using nouns and verbs to constructing better sentences. Writing exercises range from the personal narrative to the persuasive essay. With this practice, your child will gain extra confidence as he or she works on daily school lessons or standardized tests.

A thorough answer key is also provided to check the quality of answers.

A Step Toward Success

Practice may not always make perfect, but it is certainly a step in the right direction. The activities in *Core Skills: Language Arts* are an excellent way to ensure greater success for your child.

Common Nouns and Proper Nouns

A **noun** is a word that names a person, place, thing, or idea.
A **common noun** names any person, place, thing, or idea.
Examples:
    chemist, country, award
A **proper noun** names a particular person, place, thing, or idea. Notice that some proper nouns have more than one word.
Examples:
    Alfred Nobel, Sweden, Nobel Prize, Federalism

DIRECTIONS ▷ Underline the common nouns, and circle the proper nouns in each sentence.

1. Uncle Harry enjoys mysteries more than other kinds of books.
2. He stayed up all night to finish *The Hound of the Baskervilles.*
3. This scary tale was written in 1902 by Sir Arthur Conan Doyle.
4. Doyle created the famous, fictional character Sherlock Holmes.
5. Our whole class read the book *Encyclopedia Brown Carries On.*
6. Encyclopedia Brown is the funniest detective.
7. Afterwards, the shelves of the library that held mysteries were practically empty!
8. Mom had to drive me to Lexington to go to the library there.

DIRECTIONS ▷ Write a common noun to replace the proper noun. Then, write a sentence using the common noun.

9. Solitaire _Card games. I like to play card games before bed._

10. Sojourner Truth _____

11. the Boston Celtics _the basketball team. I have dreampt of being on the basketball team._

DIRECTIONS ▷ Write a proper noun to replace the common noun. Then, write a sentence using the proper noun.

12. singer _Shania Twain is a good but short singer._

13. country _Germany is my dream vacation place._

Collective Nouns and Mass Nouns

A **collective noun** is a common noun that names a group with more than one member.
Examples:
> jury, brigade, staff

A **mass noun** is a common noun that cannot be easily separated into countable units.
Examples:
> water, sand, wood, air, gold, cement

DIRECTIONS ▶ Underline the collective nouns in the sentences.

1. Flocks of penguins live only in the Southern Hemisphere.
2. Many scientific groups have studied the birds carefully.
3. A committee of biologists is studying the penguins living in New Zealand.
4. The scientists are developing a large collection of facts about the unusual birds.
5. They plan to give talks to science classes at the high school.
6. A large crowd is expected.

DIRECTIONS ▶ Write sentences using the collective nouns.

7. company _____

8. family _____

9. crowd _____

DIRECTIONS ▶ Underline the mass nouns in the sentences.

10. When you go to the grocery, don't forget the bread.
11. Get a large jar of grape jelly, too.
12. My best friend is allergic to the pollen from oak trees.
13. This fine, yellow dust can cover sidewalks and fill gutters.
14. The thunderstorm covered our town with a flood of rain.
15. All students were delighted when the school's electricity went out.

DIRECTIONS ▶ Write sentences using the mass nouns.

16. grass _____

17. oxygen _____

18. toothpaste _____

Pronouns

A **pronoun** is a word that takes the place of one or more than one noun. Pronouns show number and gender.

Number tells whether a pronoun is singular or plural.

Gender tells whether a pronoun is masculine, feminine, or neuter.

Examples:

Noun	Pronoun	Number and Gender
Bill McCoy heard	*He* heard	singular, masculine
a *librarian* tell	*her* tell	singular, feminine
stories.	*them.*	plural, neuter

Using pronouns helps writers avoid repeating the same noun over and over.

◎ ◎◎ ◎ ◎◎ ◎◎◎◎ ◎◎◎ ◎ ◎◎ ◎ ◎◎◎◎ ◎◎◎◎ ◎ ◎◎◎ ◎◎◎ ◎◎ ◎◎ ◎ ◎

DIRECTIONS ▷ **Write the pronoun from each sentence. Then, write the noun that each pronoun refers to.**

1. When Marie Dorion went with the trappers to Oregon, they showed the young woman great respect. _____

2. Marie loved Pierre Dorion and agreed to travel with him to the wild new territory.
_____

3. The couple had two sons, and they grew into big, strong boys.
_____

4. One bitter winter brought a violent snowstorm, and it trapped the young family for 53 days.
_____

5. Marie and Pierre promised the boys that they would survive.
_____

DIRECTIONS ▷ **Underline the pronouns in the sentences. Write the number and gender of each one.**

6. Leon asked Anne to tell him about some of her favorite books. _____

7. Anne chose some books and opened them. _____

8. "Biographies about women pioneers are interesting. I could talk about one of them." _____
_____

9. Leon told her to pick one. _____

10. He was surprised at her choice. _____

Subject, Object, and Possessive Pronouns

A **subject pronoun** acts as the subject of a sentence or as a predicate nominative.
Subject pronouns: I, you, he, she, it, we, they
Example:
>   *The frightened mother* dialed 9-1-1. *She* dialed 9-1-1.

An **object pronoun** can be a direct object, an indirect object, or an object of a preposition.
Object pronouns: me, you, him, her, it, us, them
Example:
>   The operator told *the woman* to stay calm. The operator told *her* to stay calm.

A **possessive pronoun** shows ownership. It takes the place of a possessive noun.
Possessive pronouns: my, mine, your, yours, his, her, hers, its, our, ours, their, theirs
Example:
>   *Selena's* dream was to be a Latina diva. *Her* dream was to be a Latina diva.

DIRECTIONS ▸ Underline the pronoun in each sentence. Then, identify it by writing *subject, object, or possessive* on the line.

1. When Monica got caught in the storm, she was careful to drive slowly. _____

2. Monica's younger brothers were with her. _____

3. Because of its icy surface, the highway was becoming dangerous. _____

4. Monica drove slowly, but she still lost control. _____

5. Bobby and Jerome got scared, and they started crying. _____

6. When the children began to wail, Monica became impatient with them. _____

7. "We must stay calm!" Monica ordered. _____

8. Her voice was shaking with tension. _____

DIRECTIONS ▸ Write *subject, object,* or *possessive* to identify each pronoun. Then, use each pronoun correctly in a sentence.

9. I _____

_____

10. their _____

_____

11. him _____

_____

Demonstrative, Indefinite, Interrogative, and Reflexive Pronouns

A **demonstrative pronoun** points out particular persons, places, or things. The demonstrative pronouns are *this, these, that, those.*
Example:
   That will be a difficult assignment.
An **indefinite pronoun** points out persons, places, or things, but less clearly than demonstrative pronouns do. Some common indefinite pronouns are *anything, no one, all, some,* and *several.*
Example:
   Not *everyone* will like the new rules.
An **interrogative pronoun** asks a question. The interrogative pronouns are *who, whom, whose, what,* and *which* when they are used to ask a question.
Example:
   Who put the dogs outside?
A **reflexive pronoun** ends in *self* or *selves.* Reflexive pronouns refer back to the subject of the sentence.
Example:
   My puppy entertains *himself* by chasing his tail.

◎ ◎ ◎◎ ◎ ◎◎ ◎◎◎ ◎ ◎◎ ◎ ◎ ◎ ◎◎ ◎ ◎ ◎ ◎◎ ◎ ◎ ◎ ◎ ◎ ◎ ◎◎◎ ◎◎ ◎ ◎ ◎ ◎ ◎ ◎ ◎ ◎ ◎ ◎

DIRECTIONS ▷ **Underline the pronoun in each sentence. Then, identify it by writing** *demonstrative, interrogative, indefinite,* **or** *reflexive* **on the line.**

_____ **1.** These are examples of Early American samplers.

_____ **2.** Olivia collected the samplers herself over the last 20 years.

_____ **3.** Everyone comments on the beauty of the materials and colors.

_____ **4.** Which does Olivia like best?

_____ **5.** Olivia likes everything in the collection.

_____ **6.** Study the samplers carefully because each portrays a specific theme.

_____ **7.** That was stitched by a seven-year-old named Hannah.

_____ **8.** The sampler itself reveals Hannah's thoughts.

_____ **9.** What is Hannah thinking about?

_____ **10.** No one knows for sure.

Action Verbs and Linking Verbs

Verbs express action or being. An **action verb** expresses physical or mental action. It tells what the subject of a sentence does or did.

Examples:

The curtain to the great stage *opens* slowly.

A **linking verb** expresses a state of being. It links the subject of a sentence with words that either describe the subject or rename it. The most common linking verb is *be*. Some forms of *be* are *am, is, are, was,* and *were*.

Examples:

The stage sets *are* superb. The stage *is* a delight to the senses.

Other common linking verbs are *seem, feel, appear, look, become, smell, taste,* and *grow*.

Examples:

The audience *grows* quiet. They *seem* to be spellbound.

DIRECTIONS ▷ Underline the verb or verbs in each sentence. Then, write *action* or *linking* on the line.

1. In general, pigs struggle with a bad reputation. _____

2. To many people, pigs seem lazy, stupid, and dirty. _____

3. Pigs grunt and wallow in the mud all day, right? _____

4. Actually, pigs are very intelligent animals. _____

5. My best friend at school adores pigs. _____

6. He brought his piglet into homeroom one day. _____

7. While it cruised the classroom, the pig oinked loudly. _____

8. Then, it ate Amy Sutton's lunch—paper bag and all. _____

9. Afterwards, the pig looked surprised at the uproar. _____

10. Fortunately, Amy seemed OK with the loss of her lunch. _____

DIRECTIONS ▷ Write *action* or *linking* to identify each verb. Then, use the verb correctly in a sentence.

11. become _____

_____

12. repair _____

_____

Main Verbs and Helping Verbs

A **verb phrase** contains one **main verb** and one or more **helping verbs**.
A **main verb** expresses the action or state of being in the sentence.
Example:
>   I have *read* some boring books lately.

A **helping verb** (auxiliary verb) helps the main verb express the action more precisely. The most common helping verbs are forms of *be, do,* and *have*. Other helping verbs include *can, may,* and *will*. A main verb can have more than one helping verb.
Examples:
>   I *have* read some boring books lately.   They *have been putting* me to sleep.

Main verbs are always the last word of a verb phrase. Helping verbs always precede the main verb. Sometimes a verb phrase is interrupted by another part of speech.
Example:
>   I will *never* finish the book at this rate.

DIRECTIONS Underline each verb phrase. Write the main and helping verbs on the lines.

1. You may know about the job of ghostwriter.

   main: _____   helping: _____

2. Ghostwriters do not haunt anyone.

   main: _____   helping: _____

3. They can help amateur writers with their manuscripts.

   main: _____   helping: _____

4. Ghostwriters have helped create some famous books.

   main: _____   helping: _____

5. You might not know the real writer of *The Personal Memoirs of Ulysses S. Grant*.

   main: _____   helping: _____

6. Grant had dictated his life story to a secretary.

   main: _____   helping: _____

7. Mark Twain, the author, may have polished it.

   main: _____   helping: _____

8. That would make Twain, in effect, the ghostwriter.

   main: _____   helping: _____

DIRECTIONS Add a helping verb to each sentence below.

9. If I _____ find a ghostwriter, I might write a book myself.

10. I wonder how much a ghostwriter _____ charge.

Verb Tenses: Present, Past, and Future

The **tense** of a verb shows time. Verb tenses change to indicate that events happen at different times. The simple tenses are the *present, past,* and the *future.*
Present tense shows action that happens now or action that happens over and over.
Past tense tells that something took place in the past. The action is over. **Future tense** tells that something will happen in the future. Add *will* to the main verb to form the future tense.
Examples:

> Jason *laughs* at Grandpa's silly story. Yesterday, he *laughed* for five minutes without a rest. Probably Jason *will laugh* at Grandpa's next story, too.

DIRECTIONS ▷ Underline the verb or verbs in each sentence. Then, write *present, past,* or *future* on the line.

1. My grandparents act in community theater productions. _____

2. Tomorrow, they will practice for four hours. _____

3. I always memorize their lines and test them. _____

4. Last night, they invited me to a rehearsal of their new play. _____

5. Ruth Rosen created and will direct *The Lines Punched Back.* _____

6. The baseball league continues to add strong new teams. _____

7. Our team will face its biggest challenge today. _____

8. The players field the ball well, but we lost the last game anyway. _____

9. Mary pitched seven innings last time, and she will be our starting pitcher today. _____

10. Will the coach replace her before the game is over? _____

DIRECTIONS ▷ Write a sentence with each verb. Use the tense given in parentheses.

11. wander (past) _____

_____

12. explore (future) _____

_____

13. observe (present) _____

_____

14. indicate (future) _____

_____

Verb Tenses: Present Perfect, Past Perfect, and Future Perfect

The **perfect tense** of a verb shows the continuation or completion of an action. The three perfect tenses are: *present perfect, past perfect,* and *future perfect.* To form the perfect tenses, use the past participle of the verb and a form of the helping verb *have.*
Present perfect tense shows action that started to happen sometime before now or action that is still happening.
Example:
> Mr. Lee *has started* the rehearsal already.

Past perfect tense shows action that happened before another past action.
Example:
> By third period, I *had planned* my entire act.

Future perfect tense shows action that will be completed before a stated time in the future.
Example:
> I *will have finished* my audition before class is over.

DIRECTIONS ▷ **Complete each sentence. Use the main verb and the verb tense identified in parentheses.**

1. (*paint*, present perfect) Believe it or not, the famous Pablo Picasso _____ on paper bags.

2. (*develop*, past perfect) Before that, most paper bag art _____ from kindergarten projects.

3. (*exist*, present perfect) Brown paper bags _____ for only 100 years.

4. (*achieve*, present perfect) Charles Stilwell _____ his place in history as the inventor of the brown paper bag.

5. (*carry*, past perfect) Before Stilwell's time, people _____ baskets when they shopped.

6. (*improve*, present perfect) Stilwell's invention, strong, stackable, and able to stand alone, _____ shopping convenience significantly.

7. (*earn*, future perfect) With a revolutionary idea like Stilwell's, someday I _____ a fortune!

8. (*start*, past perfect) If only I _____ on it earlier.

Transitive Verbs and Intransitive Verbs

A **transitive verb** is an action verb that is followed by a noun or pronoun. The noun or pronoun receives the action expressed in the verb and is called a *direct object*.
Examples:
> During the Middle Ages, blacksmiths *repaired* tools and *forged* new weapons.

Intransitive verbs include all linking verbs. Action verbs that do not have a direct object are also intransitive verbs.
Examples:
> The cart of the hot dog vendor *was* in flames. (linking verb)
> The pedestrians *stopped* and *stared*. (action verbs without a direct object)

DIRECTIONS > Underline the verbs in the sentences. Write *transitive* or *intransitive* on the line.

1. Greyfriars Bobby was a Skye terrier. _____

2. Bobby and his master, Auld Jock, lived in the hills outside Edinburgh. _____

3. The loyal animal loved Auld Jock intensely. _____

4. Auld Jock showed his dog great kindness. _____

5. One winter, Auld Jock suddenly died. _____

6. His friends gave him a funeral service in Greyfriars Churchyard. _____

7. Bobby was utterly grief-stricken. _____

8. The day after the service, the churchyard caretaker stopped and stared. _____

9. Greyfriars Bobby had found a home on top of Jock's grave. _____

10. Every day, an innkeeper and his wife brought food to the churchyard. _____

11. The people of Edinburgh told the story of Greyfriars Bobby. _____

12. Bobby gave a friendly wag of his tail to churchyard visitors. _____

DIRECTIONS > Write two sentences for each verb. In the first sentence, use the verb as an intransitive verb. In the second sentence, use the verb as a transitive verb. Sentences may be written in any of the verb tenses you know: *present, past, future,* or any of the *perfect* tenses.

13. to surprise   Intransitive: _____

    Transitive: _____

14. to tell   Intransitive: _____

    Transitive: _____

The Principal Parts of Verbs

The four basic forms of a verb are its principal parts: the **present**, the **present participle**, the **past**, and the **past participle**.

A **participle** is the form a verb takes when it is combined with a helping verb such as *be* or *have*. For regular verbs, the **present participle** is formed by adding *ing* to the present. *Examples:*

disappear   (is, are, am) disappearing

For regular verbs, the **past** is formed by adding *ed* or *d* to the present. The **past participle** is formed when a helping verb such as *have* is added to the past. *Examples:*

disappeared   (has, have, had) disappeared

The four parts of a few verbs are shown below.

Present	Present Participle	Past	Past Participle
repeat	(is, are, am) repeating	repeated	(has, have, had) repeated
suggest	(is, are, am) suggesting	suggested	(has, have, had) suggested
continue	(is, are, am) continuing	continued	(has, have, had) continued
investigate	(is, are, am) investigating	investigated	(has, have, had) investigated

◎ ◎ ◎◎ ◎ ◎◎ ◎ ◎◎◎ ◎ ◎◎ ◎ ◎◎◎ ◎ ◎◎ ◎ ◎◎◎ ◎ ◎◎◎ ◎ ◎◎◎ ◎ ◎◎ ◎ ◎ ◎

DIRECTIONS ▷ **Write the correct form of the verb in parentheses.**

1. (*jog*, present) Every year, runners _____ for miles in the Boston Marathon.

2. (*race*, past participle) Drivers _____ sleek cars around the track at the Indianapolis 500 for years.

3. (*follow*, present participle) But in Alaska this March, the runners _____ along behind dog sleds.

4. (*extend*, present) The 1,000-mile course of the Iditarod Sled Dog Race _____ from Anchorage to Nome.

5. (*commemorate*, present) The Iditarod race _____ a real-life race against death.

6. (*start*, past participle) By the winter of 1925, the Alaskan Gold Rush _____ .

7. (*threaten*, past) Suddenly, an epidemic of diphtheria _____ Nome.

8. (*carry*, past) A relay of brave dog sledders _____ lifesaving serum form Anchorage to Nome.

9. (*try*, present participle) This year, dozens of dog sledders _____ to recreate the famous rescue.

◎ ◎◎ ◎ ◎◎ ◎ ◎◎◎ ◎ ◎◎ ◎ ◎◎◎ ◎ ◎◎ ◎ ◎◎ ◎ ◎◎◎ ◎ ◎◎ ◎ ◎◎◎ ◎ ◎◎ ◎

Irregular Verbs

Form the past tense of regular verbs by adding *ed* or *d* to the end of the word. Form the past participle of a regular verb by adding *have, has,* or *had* to the past tense. The past tense and past participle of an **irregular verb** do not end in *ed* or *d*. You must memorize the past tense and past participle of irregular verbs. Three parts of a few irregular verbs are shown below.

Present	Past	Past Participle
begin	began	begun
forget	forgot	forgotten
go	went	gone
write	wrote	written

Dictionaries always include the past and past participle forms of verbs.

DIRECTIONS ▷ **Write the correct form of the verb in parentheses.**

1. (take) Termites have _____ over our home.

2. (know) I wish I had _____ they made such lousy pets.

3. (get) Those termites have _____ some delicious, wooden meals at my house.

4. (grow) Each disgusting bug has _____ to a shocking size.

5. (wear) Some even have _____ my husband's ties.

6. (ride) Yesterday, my youngest child _____ one around the porch.

7. (choose) Last winter, the termites _____ to eat the north wall.

8. (freeze) We almost _____ before the spring came.

DIRECTIONS ▷ **Find the error or errors in each sentence. Write the sentence correctly.**

9. Celia has came to the family reunion for five years. _____

_____

10. Her chauffeur brung her this year because she had a broken arm. _____

_____

11. Paolo driven up to the entrance in a big, black limo. _____

_____

12. The entire family seen Celia's grand arrival. _____

Adjectives

Adjectives modify, or describe, nouns or pronouns. Adjectives tell *what kind, how many,* or *which one.*
Examples:

The *gentle* purr of the *two* kittens was the *last* sound I heard.

The adjectives *a, an,* and *the* are called **articles**. Use *a* before a word that begins with a consonant. Use *an* before a word that begins with a vowel.
Examples:

A kitten can develop into *a* cat with *an* attitude.

A **proper adjective** is a word that is formed from a proper noun. A proper adjective always begins with a capital letter.
Examples:

Albert Schweitzer was a *German* doctor who worked in *African* hospitals.

Skilled writers use adjectives to make sentences more **vivid**.
Examples:

The library has a collection of scrolls.
The library has *an immense* collection of *ancient* scrolls.

DIRECTIONS Underline the adjectives in each sentence, except the articles (*a, an, the*). Then, write the nouns they modify.

1. The powerful lion is actually a sociable creature. _____

2. Mischievous cubs are taught important skills by watchful adults. _____

3. In ancient times, lions roamed the grassy areas of Europe and India. _____

4. Today, only two hundred lions still live in Asia. _____

DIRECTIONS Underline each adjective once. Underline each proper adjective twice. Circle each article.

5. A British guide accompanied us on a tour of the Mediterranean area.

6. Fortunately, the English language is spoken in most countries.

7. The African nations that border the sea are fascinating countries.

8. Seeing the Egyptian pyramids was an unforgettable experience.

DIRECTIONS Rewrite the sentence, adding vivid adjectives.

9. I saw a caterpillar munching a leaf in a tree. _____

_____

More About Adjectives

Demonstrative adjectives point out a noun. The words *this, that, these,* and *those* are demonstrative adjectives. Demonstrative adjectives are more precise than articles because they tell which one.

Examples:

>*This* book has more illustrations than *that* magazine.

Demonstrative adjectives always modify a noun. Demonstrative pronouns (page 9) replace a noun rather than modifying it.

Examples:

>*That* assignment will be difficult. (adjective)

>*That* will be a difficult assignment. (pronoun)

Nouns, pronouns, and verbs can be used as adjectives because the way a word is used determines its part of speech.

Examples:

>*Our* family has always run a farm. Today, *family* farms have a hard time surviving. *Farming* equipment is costly.

DIRECTIONS ▷ **Underline the demonstrative adjectives and pronouns. Write *adjective* or *pronoun* on the line. Rewrite each sentence, changing demonstrative adjectives to pronouns and vice versa.**

1. Those are my favorite books. _____

_____

2. This collection of African instruments is magnificent. _____

_____

3. These instruments are called *kalimbas*, or "thumb pianos." _____

_____

4. This is a superior example of early African artistry. _____

_____

DIRECTIONS ▷ **Identify the part of speech of each underlined word. Circle N for noun, P for pronoun, A for adjective, or V for verb.**

5. The number of large <u>factory</u> farms is increasing.   N   P   A   V

6. Factory farms keep hundreds of <u>roosting</u> chickens cooped up together.   N   P   A   V

7. <u>This</u> practice requires that all the chickens be debeaked and fed antibiotics.   N   P   A   V

8. <u>Bright</u> lights burn all day to encourage the hens to lay eggs.   N   P   A   V

Comparing with Adjectives

An adjective has three degrees of comparison: **positive**, **comparative**, and **superlative**.
A **positive adjective** is used when no comparison is being made.
Examples:

How *old* the Inca empire seems! How *ancient* the Inca empire seems!

A **comparative adjective** is used to compare two items. Form the comparative of most one-syllable adjectives by adding *er*. For most adjectives with two or more syllables, add the word *more* before the adjective.
Examples:

The Aztec empire is *older* than the Inca empire.

The Aztec empire is *more ancient* than the Inca empire.

A **superlative adjective** is used to compare three or more items. Form the superlative of most one-syllable adjectives by adding *est*. For most adjectives with two or more syllables, add the word *most* before the adjective.
Examples:

The Mayan empire is the *oldest* one in the Americas.

The Mayan empire is the *most ancient* one in the Americas.

Some adjectives have special forms for comparing.
Example:

good, better, best

DIRECTIONS Write the correct form of the adjective in parentheses. Then, write *positive, comparative,* or *superlative* to identify the degree of comparison.

1. (strange) Which is _____, truth or fiction? _____

2. (reliable) Thousands of _____ witnesses have reported seeing aliens from outer space. _____

3. (weird) One of the _____ of all insects is the female praying mantis, which eats its mate alive. _____

4. (long) The tubes in just one of your kidneys are much _____ than your trip to camp—40 miles! _____

5. (amazing) Some would vote crystals the _____ things on Earth. _____

6. (unvarying) We keep time by the crystals' _____ vibrations. _____

7. (good) Which of the many students will create the _____ poster about an ancient civilization? _____

Adverbs

Adverbs modify a verb, an adjective, or another adverb. Adverbs tell *how, when, where, how often,* and *to what extent*. Many adverbs end in *ly*.
Examples:
> The joggers dressed *warmly* before they headed *outside*. (tell *how* and *where*)

Place adverbs that modify adjectives or other adverbs just before the word they modify.
Examples:
> The air was *quite* cold. The joggers hoped they would warm up *very* quickly.

Adverbs that modify verbs can be placed almost anywhere in the sentence.
Examples:
> *Suddenly,* the wind rose. The wind rose *suddenly*.

Negatives are words that mean "no," such as *not, never, nowhere, neither,* and *barely*.
Negatives often function as adverbs.
Examples:
> I can *hardly* believe that you have *never* eaten oysters.

DIRECTIONS Underline each adverb and circle the word it modifies. Write whether the adverb tells *how, when, where, how often,* or *to what extent.*

1. You may firmly believe that the existence of UFOs is a hoax. _____

2. Many nonbelievers have completely changed their minds. _____

3. More and more strange, luminous craft are being sighted overhead. _____

4. Weather balloons and aircraft fool people sometimes. _____

5. Some people will never be convinced. _____

DIRECTIONS Circle the word that the underlined adverb modifies. Write *verb, adjective,* or *adverb* on the line.

6. The serious surfers arrive <u>first</u> on the beach. _____

7. They are <u>most</u> likely to be in the water by 5:30 A.M. _____

8. Lifeguards watch the swimmers <u>carefully</u>. _____

9. A strong undertow can be <u>very</u> dangerous. _____

10. Lifeguards shouted <u>very</u> loudly to those in the water. _____

11. Our lifeguard warned the swimmer <u>sternly</u>. _____

12. Some swimmers can be <u>rather</u> careless. _____

13. Smart swimmers <u>always</u> observe the rules. _____

Comparing with Adverbs

Adverbs can be used to compare two or more actions. A **positive adverb** is used when no comparison is being made.
Examples:

      I studied *hard* for the test. Snow falls *frequently* in Vermont.

A **comparative adverb** is used to compare two actions. Form the comparative by adding *er* to the positive form or by placing the word *more* or *less* before the adverb.
Examples:

      I must study *harder* this year than last year. Snow comes *more frequently* when the wind is from the north.

A **superlative adverb** compares three or more actions. Form the superlative by adding *est* to the positive form or by placing the word *most* or *least* before the adverb.
Examples:

      I will study *hardest* for final exams. Snow comes *most frequently* during February.

Some adverbs have special forms for comparing.
Example:

      badly, worse, worst

DIRECTIONS The underlined words are adverbs. Write *positive, comparative,* or *superlative* to identify the degree of comparison.

1. Rainstorms <u>commonly</u> occur in cities like Seattle that are close to the ocean. _____

2. In which areas of the world are rainstorms <u>most likely</u> to occur? _____

3. Scientists tell us that rainstorms occur <u>more frequently</u> in tropical climates than in temperate zones. _____

4. It seems to rain <u>constantly</u> in the forests of Central America. _____

5. Clouds fill with moisture <u>more readily</u> over water than over land. _____

6. If you don't like rainstorms, it is <u>better</u> to live inland than on the coast. _____

7. The <u>worst</u> place of all for severe weather would be an island in the South Pacific. _____

DIRECTIONS Write your own adverb to complete each sentence. Use the degree of comparison indicated in parentheses.

8. (positive) Celia yearns _____ to go to high school.

9. (comparative) Her brother, who is a junior, does _____ than Celia on report cards.

10. (comparative) Celia is _____ interested in football games than report cards.

Adverb or Adjective?

Adverbs modify verbs, adjectives, or other adverbs. Adjectives modify nouns and pronouns.
Examples:
> We may never know the *real* facts in the case. (adjective)
> We may never *really* know the facts in the case. (adverb)

The words *good* and *well* are often confused. *Good* is an adjective and, therefore, always modifies a noun or pronoun.
Example:
> A *good* book and a rainy day are a great combination.

Well is usually an adverb used to tell how something is done. *Well* is an adjective only when it means "healthy."
Examples:
> Jesse is doing *well* after the surgery. (adjective)
> The surgery went *well*. (adverb)

DIRECTIONS ▷ **Write the word in parentheses that completes each sentence correctly. Write *adjective* or *adverb* on the line.**

1. (strange, strangely) Some _____ stones stand in Salisbury, England.

_____

2. (strange, strangely) From a distance, they seem to hang _____ in the air.

_____

3. (unusual, unusually) They are the _____ Standing Stones of Stonehenge.

_____

4. (unusual, unusually) Their mystery has been _____ difficult to solve.

_____

5. (immense, immensely) Many of the stones are _____. _____

6. (immense, immensely) Scientists find it _____ difficult to explain how they

got there. _____

7. (good, well) The passing years have hidden Stonehenge's purpose _____.

_____

8. (good, well) The mystery of Stonehenge would be a _____ subject for a

report. _____

Prepositions and Prepositional Phrases

A **preposition** shows the relationship of a noun or pronoun to some other word or words in a sentence. Common prepositions include *about, with, in, for, to,* and *of.*
Example:
> The average four-year-old asks 437 questions *during* a single day.

An **object of a preposition** is the noun or pronoun that follows a preposition.
Example:
> The average four-year-old asks 437 questions during a single *day*.

A **prepositional phrase** is made up of a preposition, the object of the preposition, and all the words in between.
Example:
> The average four-year-old asks 437 questions *during a single day*.

DIRECTIONS The underlined word in each sentence is the object of the proposition. Write the preposition for each object on the line.

1. The rudder, the single mast, and the compass were all invented by the <u>Chinese</u>. _____

2. Can you imagine steering a boat without a <u>rudder</u>? _____

3. The compass made navigation through foggy and dark <u>nights</u> possible. _____

4. The compass was first mentioned in a <u>book</u> dated 1117. _____

5. The compass was actually invented at a much earlier <u>date</u>. _____

DIRECTIONS These sentences contain two prepositional phrases. Underline the first phrase, and circle the second one.

6. The average elevator in an office building travels about 10,000 miles during one year.

7. Some students believe that lying down with pillows under their feet helps them solve math problems.

8. The average American drinks about 28,000 quarts of milk in a lifetime.

9. Many passengers leaned over the railings of the large ship.

10. Visitors began to walk down the gangplank and onto the dock.

11. The ship would soon be sailing beneath an overcast sky into the cold Atlantic Ocean.

12. The young girl stood silently among the strangers and thought about her new life.

Prepositional Phrases Used as Adjectives and Adverbs

A prepositional phrase that modifies a noun or pronoun is functioning as an **adjective phrase**. Remember that adjectives tell *what kind, how many,* or *which one.*

A prepositional phrase that modifies a verb, adjective, or another adverb is functioning as an **adverb phrase**. Remember that adverbs tell *how, when, where, how often,* and *to what extent.*

Examples:

The whale *with the unusual markings* is our favorite.
(adjective phrase; tells which whale)

The whales in the water park show performed *with ease.*
(adverb phrase; tells how)

DIRECTIONS ▷ Underline the adjective phrase in each sentence. Write the word it modifies.

1. Horseshoe crabs resemble hard hats with long tails. _____

2. They are close relatives of spiders. _____

3. The mouth of the horseshoe crab is well hidden. _____

4. It is an opening underneath the crab's body. _____

DIRECTIONS ▷ Underline the adverb phrase in each sentence. Write the word(s) it modifies.

5. Whales are the largest mammals that live on the Earth. _____

6. Whales behave with great intelligence. _____

7. A whale must breathe air through its lungs. _____

8. Whales can dive for long periods. _____

DIRECTIONS ▷ Underline each prepositional phrase. Then, circle *ADJ* for adjective phrases or *ADV* for adverb phrases.

9. One rock sample from the moon is 4,720 million years old.   ADJ   ADV

10. The rock was collected by the Apollo space mission.   ADJ   ADV

11. The daytime temperature on the lunar equator is 243°F.   ADJ   ADV

12. A black hole is formed by a star's complete collapse.   ADJ   ADV

13. About 150 meteorites from space pound the Earth each year.   ADJ   ADV

14. An Alaskan, Mrs. E. H. Hodges, is the only person hurt by a falling meteorite.   ADJ   ADV

Conjunctions

Conjunctions connect words or word groups. The **coordinating conjunctions** *and, but,* and *or* join ideas that are similar. The **correlative conjunctions** (*either/or, neither/nor,* and *both/and*) join pairs of ideas.
Examples:

Carelessness is the cause of many *falls and burns.*
The athletes will need *both skill and endurance* to win the playoffs.

The coordinating conjunctions *and, but, or, nor for, so,* and *yet* are used to combine two sentences that are related. Remember to place a comma before the conjunction when you write sentences this way.
Example:

Craig gets into trouble, *but* he usually gets out of it.

DIRECTIONS ▷ **Underline each conjunction. Write *coordinating* or *correlative* on the line.**

1. Neither Antonio nor I have ever seen a carnivorous plant. _____

2. Today, we went walking in the woods behind my house and saw something unusual. _____

3. We thought it was a pitcher plant, but we weren't sure. _____

4. Back at home, we researched pitcher plants and learned more about them. _____

5. Most pitcher plants live in bogs or wetlands. _____

6. The soil there has plenty of water but very few nutrients. _____

7. The pitcher plants must either obtain more nutrients or die. _____

8. They get their meals by trapping moths, wasps, and other bugs. _____

DIRECTIONS ▷ **Combine the two sentences using a coordinating conjunction. Remember to punctuate the new sentence correctly.**

9. Llamas are quite affectionate. They enjoy humans as company. _____

_____

10. Llamas have no natural defenses like horns. They spit to show they are mad. _____

_____

11. Llamas are tamer than farm animals. They make good pets. _____

_____

12. You can check out a book about llamas. You can research them on the Internet. _____

_____

More About Conjunctions

Subordinating conjunctions connect an independent clause with one or more dependent clauses. Some common subordinating conjunctions are *since, before,* and *unless.*
Example:

> *Because* dimples were in fashion in 1896, Martin Goetz invented a dimple-making machine.

Sometimes adverbs, such as *however,* are used as conjunctions. They are used to connect two independent clauses to form a compound sentence.
Example:

> Rainy weather is common in Seattle; *however,* most people don't mind it.

DIRECTIONS ▷ **Write the subordinating conjunction on the line.**

1. If you go to New York City, consider a visit to Brooklyn. _____

2. Fifteen teenagers there gained some fame because they were pollution fighters. _____

3. They called themselves the Toxic Avengers since that is the name of a pollution-fighting superhero. _____

4. Although it was located next to a school, the Radiac Research Corporation was storing large amounts of medical waste. _____

5. When the Toxic Avengers learned about this, they planned a rally. _____

6. Public awareness grew after the rally was held. _____

DIRECTIONS ▷ **Connect the two sentences with an adverb from the box below. Write the new sentence on the line.**

consequently	still	further	thus	however	therefore	**WORD BOX**
nevertheless	also	besides	then	moreover	otherwise	

7. Frank had painted a lot of rooms. He needed the money. _____

_____

8. He knew the work would be dirty and exhausting. The price was right. _____

_____

9. Frank scrubbed hard for two hours. The walls were free of dirt. _____

_____

10. The paint on one wall was thin. He never would have noticed something beneath the surface.

_____

Interjections

An **interjection** is a word or group of words that expresses strong feeling. Place an exclamation point following the interjection if it is used to express strong emotion. Express milder emotions by placing a comma between the interjection and the rest of the sentence.

Examples:

> *Well,* Snoopy is at the typewriter again.
> *Rats!* I hope he doesn't write another letter to the president!

DIRECTIONS > **Add the correct punctuation to these sentences with interjections. Underline any words that should be capitalized.**

1. Say you're not superstitious, are you?

2. Really no one believes in that silly stuff anymore.

3. Ouch I broke a mirror and cut my finger.

4. Oh no some people believe that's seven years' bad luck.

5. Hey we thought you didn't believe in superstitions.

6. Oops well it doesn't hurt to be careful.

DIRECTIONS > **Add an interjection to each sentence.**

7. _____! Harry certainly is superstitious!

8. _____, I never knew that.

9. _____, he has more superstitions than anyone I know.

10. _____, did you know Harry believes that running around his house three times will improve his luck?

11. _____! He never gets out of bed on the left side because it's very bad luck.

12. _____, he also thinks wearing clothes wrong side out brings good luck.

DIRECTIONS > **Write sentences using the following interjections: *bravo, ssh,* and *awesome*.**

13. _____

14. _____

15. _____

Infinitives and Infinitive Phrases

An **infinitive** is a verb that functions as a noun or adjective. The word *to* precedes the verb in an infinitive.
Example:
> Someday, I would like *to write* beautiful poetry.

An **infinitive phrase** includes the infinitive, its object, and the object's modifiers.
Examples:
> Someday, I would like *to write beautiful poetry*.

Readers sometimes confuse infinitives with prepositional phrases that begin with *to*. Remember that a verb follows *to* in an infinitive phrase. A noun or pronoun follows *to* in a prepositional phrase.

◎ ◎ ◎◎ ◎◎ ◎◎◎ ◎◎◎ ◎◎◎ ◎◎◎ ◎◎◎ ◎◎◎ ◎◎◎ ◎◎◎ ◎◎ ◎◎ ◎

> **DIRECTIONS** Underline the infinitive phrase in each sentence.

1. I like to work in my garden.
2. Each spring I wait impatiently to see my garden reappear.
3. I select special flowers to attract hummingbirds.
4. Perennials are the flowers I choose to grow.

> **DIRECTIONS** The underlined words are parts of infinitive phrases. Write *infinitive*, *object*, or *modifier* on the line.

5. You don't have to plant <u>perennials</u> every year, as you do annuals. _____

6. Gardeners need <u>to think</u> about the time each perennial will bloom. _____

7. I don't need to tell <u>you</u> how satisfying a beautiful garden can be. _____

8. To have a <u>beautiful</u> garden, you must plan, dig, weed, and rearrange constantly. _____

> **DIRECTIONS** Expand the infinitives by adding an object or modifier. Then, write a sentence using the expanded phrase.

9. to encourage   expanded phrase: _____

   Sentence: _____

10. to protest   expanded phrase: _____

   Sentence: _____

11. to conceal   expanded phrase: _____

   Sentence: _____

Gerunds and Gerund Phrases

A **gerund** is a verb that ends in *ing* and functions as a noun.
Example:

> *Estimating* is an important mathematics skill.

A **gerund phrase** includes the gerund, its object, and the object's modifiers.
Example:

> *Writing a best seller* is the goal of every novelist.

Because gerunds function as nouns, they have many uses. Gerunds can be the subject of a sentence, a direct object, and the object of a preposition.

DIRECTIONS ▷ **Underline the gerund phrase in each sentence.**

1. Running long distances is no problem for me.
2. My goal is jogging about three miles per day.
3. Giving in to aches and pains is not an option.
4. As they run along, some people enjoy reciting a favorite poem.
5. Refusing to quit is a characteristic of good runners.

DIRECTIONS ▷ **The underlined words are parts of gerund phrases. Write *gerund*, *object*, or *modifier* on the line.**

6. I like <u>jogging</u> along the seashore best. _____

7. Breathing <u>deeply</u> is easier out in the fresh air. _____

8. Feeling the <u>crisp</u> wind on my face is a unique experience. _____

9. Sometimes, I use <u>singing</u> as a way to keep going. _____

10. Running a <u>marathon</u> next year is my New Year's resolution. _____

DIRECTIONS ▷ **Write *subject*, *direct object*, or *object of preposition* to identify how the underlined gerund functions in each sentence.**

11. <u>Disciplining</u> myself to run every day isn't as difficult as I thought. _____

12. I just concentrate on <u>winning</u> the Boston Marathon. _____

13. I like <u>looking</u> around at the world as I run. _____

14. As a matter of fact, other ways of <u>exercising</u> seem dull to me. _____

15. <u>Achieving</u> a goal is the best incentive for hard work. _____

Participles and Participial Phrases

A **participle** is a verb that functions as an adjective. Both the present and past participle forms of the verb can be used as adjectives.
Examples:

A *running* horse galloped down the road. *Dried* leaves flew from his hooves.

A **participial phrase** includes the participle, its modifier, and its objects.
Example:

The child, *flashing a mischievous smile*, turned and walked away.

DIRECTIONS Underline the participial phrase in each sentence. Write the noun or pronoun it modifies on the line.

1. That man kicking the soccer ball is Pele. _____

2. People interested in soccer say he was the greatest player ever. _____

3. Pele's first ball was a stocking stuffed with rags. _____

4. The determined boy joined a professional team at age 15. _____

5. Racing down the field, Pele was in his element. _____

DIRECTIONS The underlined words are participles or parts of participial phrases. Write *participle*, *object*, or *modifier* on the line.

6. People interested <u>in soccer</u> say he was the greatest player ever. _____

7. A <u>record-breaking</u> crowd attended his final game in 1971. _____

8. Pele's first ball was a stocking stuffed <u>with rags</u>. _____

9. The <u>determined</u> boy joined a professional team at age 15. _____

10. The fans encircling the <u>field</u> were thrilled by his speed. _____

DIRECTIONS Create the kind of participle indicated in parentheses. Expand it by adding an object or modifier, and write the phrase on the line. Then, write a sentence using the expanded phrase.

11. protect (present participle)   expanded phrase: _____

Sentence: _____

12. write (past participle)   expanded phrase: _____

Sentence: _____

Simple Sentences and Word Order

A **sentence** expresses a complete thought. At a minimum, it must contain a subject and a verb. **Simple sentences** contain only one complete thought.

Most sentences use **natural word order**. The subject of the sentence comes first, followed by the verb and any objects. Some sentences, such as questions, have **inverted word order**. The verb, or part of it, comes first, followed by the subject.

Examples:

The reptile Plateosaurus was 25 feet long. (natural word order)

Do you think that is an exaggeration? (inverted word order)

DIRECTIONS ▷ Write *complete* or *incomplete* after each group of words to indicate whether the words express a complete thought.

1. Have you seen the Meteor Crater in Arizona? _____

2. About 4,150 feet across and about 570 feet deep. _____

3. A meteorite crashed there 50,000 years ago. _____

4. May have fallen even earlier. _____

5. In 1908, a meteorite streaked across the Siberian sky. _____

6. People could see it for hundreds of miles. _____

7. Really weigh hundreds of tons? _____

8. In 1947, another meteorite exploded over Siberia, creating more than 200 craters. _____

DIRECTIONS ▷ Rewrite the sentence fragments you identified above. Be sure each one expresses a complete thought and is punctuated correctly.

9. _____

10. _____

11. _____

DIRECTIONS ▷ Write *natural* or *inverted* to indicate the word order in each sentence.

12. High heels were first worn by men in the 1500s. _____

13. Do you know how high heels were first used? _____

14. They helped keep riders' feet in their stirrups. _____

15. Don't you assume that all footwear should include a right foot and a left foot? _____

16. Well, shoes in Colonial America were all made to fit either foot. _____

Types of Sentences

A **declarative sentence** makes a statement. Place a period at the end of a declarative sentence.

An **interrogative sentence** asks a question. Place a question mark at the end of an interrogative sentence.

An **imperative sentence** gives a command or makes a request. Place a period at the end of an imperative sentence.

An **exclamatory sentence** expresses strong feeling. Place an exclamation point at the end of an exclamatory sentence.

Examples:

> Janelle is painting a picture of an imaginary place. (*declarative* sentence)
> Who could ever create a more imaginative scene? (*interrogative* sentence)
> Plan to see her work as soon as you can. (*imperative* sentence)
> What fantastic colors she uses! (*exclamatory* sentence)

◎ ◎ ◎◎ ◎◎ ◎◎◎◎◎◎◎◎◎ ◎◎◎ ◎◎◎◎ ◎◎◎ ◎◎ ◎◎◎◎◎◎ ◎ ◎◎ ◎◎ ◎

DIRECTIONS ▷ Put the correct punctuation mark at the end of the each sentence. Then, write *declarative, interrogative, imperative,* or *exclamatory* on the line.

1. Look carefully at that photograph _____

2. How did the photographer manage to capture such an unusual shot _____

3. What an unusual background the photo has _____

4. Photographers study for years to learn to use backgrounds effectively _____

5. What skill these artists possess _____

6. Observe the shape of the object in the picture _____

7. What do you think it could possibly be _____

8. Shots like this one create an eerie sense of emptiness _____

DIRECTIONS ▷ Rewrite each sentence as the kind of sentence identified in parentheses.

9. A llama is not a wild animal. (interrogative) _____

10. You might find it interesting to research the various habitats of the llama. (imperative) _____

_____

11. Don't llamas have only two toes on each foot? (declarative) _____

_____

12. Some people think llamas are strange animals. (exclamatory) _____

◎◎◎ ◎ ◎◎ ◎ Sentences ◎◎◎ ◎◎ ◎ ◎◎◎ ◎ ◎◎◎ ◎◎◎◎ ◎◎ ◎◎◎ ◎◎ ◎◎◎ ◎◎

Complete, Simple, and Compound Subjects

The **complete subject** of a sentence includes all the words that tell who or what the sentence is about.
Example:
> *Everyone in my house* is keeping a secret.

The **simple subject** is the main word or words in the complete subject.
Example:
> *Everyone* in my house is keeping a secret.

Sometimes the complete subject and the simple subject are the same.
Example:
> *Marlon* practiced and daydreamed for weeks before the game.

A **compound subject** contains two or more subjects that have the same predicate. The simple subjects in a compound subject are usually joined by *and* or *or*.
Example:
> The *craters* and *plains* of the moon have had no human visitors for some time.

◎◎◎ ◎◎◎ ◎◎◎◎◎ ◎◎◎ ◎◎◎ ◎◎◎ ◎◎◎ ◎◎◎◎◎ ◎◎◎ ◎◎◎ ◎◎◎ ◎◎ ◎

DIRECTIONS ▷ **Underline the complete subject in each sentence. Then, write the simple subject on the line.**

1. A wooden feeder for the birds hangs outside my window. _____

2. The clear, pleasant whistles of the goldfinches often echo in the trees nearby. _____

3. Our chubby, orange kitty watches the birds from the window. _____

4. She can't figure out exactly what to do. _____

5. I feel sorry for our poor, confused feline. _____

6. *Birds of North America* helps us identify our feathered visitors. _____

7. A strong telescope can help bird-watchers see the birds from a far distance. _____

8. Even relatively small binoculars can help watchers recognize different species. _____

DIRECTIONS ▷ **Underline the compound subject in each sentence. Circle the verb.**

9. Myon and I went on a camping trip last fall.

10. Myon and his dad took charge of packing and finding a campground.

11. Myon, his dad, or I should have thought about planning for rain.

12. We and all our equipment were soaked through in the first ten minutes.

13. Our sleeping bags and down jackets looked like wet dishcloths.

14. Myon and I were wet, tired, and disappointed.

Complete, Simple, and Compound Predicates

> The **complete predicate** of a sentence includes all the words that tell what the subject does or is.
> *Example:*
> > My two older brothers *stared at me silently.*
> The **simple predicate** is the main verb in the complete predicate.
> *Example:*
> > My two older brothers *stared* at me silently.
> A **compound predicate** contains two or more predicates that have the same subject.
> The simple predicates in a compound predicate are usually joined by *and, but,* or *or.*
> *Example:*
> > We *will find* the card catalog *or will ask* the librarian for help.

DIRECTIONS ▷ **Underline the complete predicate in each sentence. Then, write the simple predicate on the line.**

1. Ralph's father put the new plants on the ground. _____

2. The two gardeners dug a separate hole for each plant. _____

3. Ralph's sister Liz watered the plants generously. _____

4. Green leaves sprouted soon on all the plants. _____

5. All of the garden's plants were growing well. _____

6. None of the plants had bloomed, though. _____

7. Ralph and Liz inspected the garden one morning. _____

8. The smallest plant of all had suddenly produced three lovely flowers! _____

DIRECTIONS ▷ **Underline the compound predicate in each sentence. Circle the subject.**

9. Alfio Carlucci came out of the house and sat on the porch.

10. He enjoyed life on the farm but was a little lonely.

11. Alfio's friends lived several miles away and rarely visited.

12. Alfio's parents had immigrated to the United States in 1998 and settled on this remote farm.

13. They had worked hard to learn English but were still embarrassed about their accents.

14. Alfio longed for his own car and daydreamed of ways to pay for it.

15. The Carluccis talked with each other in the kitchen but kept their voices soft.

16. They knew of Alfio's loneliness and planned to do something about it.

Predicate Nominatives

A **predicate nominative** is a noun or pronoun that follows a linking verb and renames the subject.
Examples:

Susan B. Anthony was an early *feminist*. (noun)

It was *she* who led the women's suffrage movement to victory. (pronoun)

Predicate nominatives sometimes contain more than one noun. These are called **compound predicate nominatives**.
Example:

Mahatma Ghandi was a Hindu religious *leader* and a social *reformer* in India.

> **DIRECTIONS**   **Write the predicate nominative from each sentence on the line. Some sentences may have a compound predicate nominative.**

1. Finland is a country with a language very different from English. _____

2. Finnish citizens, though, are people just like us. _____

3. Recently, I have become a pen pal to one of them. _____

4. Eric Hirvonen is a guy about my age. _____

5. He is a student and the son of a college professor. _____

6. The capital city of Helsinki has been his home throughout his life. _____

7. Although we are on opposite sides of the world, Eric and I are good friends. _____

8. Becoming a composer is my career choice. _____

9. Eric's goals are dancing and choreography. _____

10. Will Eric and I be friends for life? _____

11. I am not the one to decide that question. _____

12. However, people can be friends for a long time. _____

13. Eric is a person I enjoy knowing. _____

14. We hope to be visitors in each other's countries. _____

15. Our visits would be happy experiences. _____

16. Such experiences are memories we would enjoy. _____

Predicate Adjectives

A **predicate adjective** is an adjective that follows a linking verb and modifies the subject of a sentence.
Example:
> A freshly baked pie is *delightful* to the eye and nose.

Predicate adjectives sometimes contain more than one adjective. These are called **compound predicate adjectives**.
Example:
> The job applicant seems *honest* and *reliable*.

◎◎ ◎◎ ◎◎ ◎◎◎ ◎◎◎ ◎◎◎ ◎◎◎ ◎◎◎ ◎◎ ◎◎◎ ◎◎◎ ◎◎◎ ◎◎ ◎

> **DIRECTIONS** Write the predicate adjective from each sentence on the line. Some sentences may have a compound predicate adjective.

1. Columbus must have been aghast as he sailed near Bermuda. _____

2. Suddenly, the sea was alive with vegetation. _____

3. The Sargasso Sea is totally eerie, even for a courageous explorer. _____

4. The Sargasso is different from any other place on Earth. _____

5. The sea looks solid from a distance. _____

6. It is strange to see a body of water so choked with seaweed. _____

7. The Sargasso is more saline and more barren than any other area in our oceans.

_____

8. With its floating weeds, the sea is unique and therefore fascinating to scientists.

_____

9. Sailors have always been fearful of the Sargasso. _____

> **DIRECTIONS** Write two sentences with each verb. In the first sentence, use the verb as an action verb. In the second sentence, use it as a linking verb with a predicate adjective.

10. taste _____

_____

11. remain _____

_____

12. grow _____

_____

◎◎ ◎◎ ◎◎ ◎◎◎ ◎◎◎ ◎◎ ◎◎◎ ◎◎◎ ◎◎◎ ◎◎◎ ◎◎◎ ◎◎ ◎

Direct Objects

A **direct object** is a noun or pronoun that follows an action verb. Direct objects tell *who* or *what* receives the action.
Example:

   I inherited a pet *deer* from the former residents of my house. (tells *what*)
   The surgical team asked *Dr. Habib* to explain the procedure. (tells *who*)

◎ ◎◎ ◎◎ ◎◎◎ ◎ ◎◎ ◎ ◎◎ ◎◎◎ ◎◎◎ ◎◎◎ ◎◎◎ ◎◎◎ ◎◎◎ ◎◎◎ ◎ ◎◎ ◎

DIRECTIONS ▶ **Underline the verb in each sentence. Then, write the direct object or objects on the line.**

1. My dad earns money catching lobsters. _____

2. He boards his boat every day at dawn. _____

3. The seagulls overhead screech a greeting. _____

4. From about a mile offshore, Dad scans the horizon. _____

5. Brightly colored buoys mark the positions of lobster traps. _____

6. He uses white paint and orange flags on his buoys. _____

7. With a winch, Dad pulls his traps up from the ocean floor. _____

8. Inside, lobsters wave their pincerlike claws back and forth. _____

9. Dad slips small wooden pegs in the claws' joints to keep them closed. _____

10. Soon, he drops the traps and the buoys back over the side of the boat. _____

11. My grandfather cooks the lobsters to perfection. _____

12. He memorized the secret, family recipe long ago. _____

DIRECTIONS ▶ **Write two sentences with each verb. In the first sentence, include a direct object that tells *what*. In the second sentence, include a direct object that tells *who*. You may use any verb tense.**

13. imagine _____

_____

14. find _____

_____

15. expect _____

_____

Indirect Objects

An **indirect object** is a noun or pronoun that follows an action verb. Indirect objects tell *to whom* or *for whom* the action of the verb is done.
For a sentence to have an indirect object, it must first have a direct object.
An indirect object is usually placed between the action verb and the direct object.
Examples:

> The vet sent *me* a reminder to bring my dogs in for their shots.
> Before we left, I gave *each dog* a warning about politeness.

DIRECTIONS ▷ **Underline the verb in each sentence. Write the direct object on the first line and the indirect object on the second.**

1. My parents promised me riding lessons at the local stable.

   _____   _____

2. My awkward attempts only won me a horse laugh from the riding mistress.

   _____   _____

3. This dictionary of horse lore offers readers some interesting trivia about horses.

   _____   _____

4. For example, a wooden horse gave the people of Troy quite a surprise.

   _____   _____

5. And many years ago, Britons fed horses chestnuts as medicine.

   _____   _____

6. Our teacher told the class the story of the mythical horse Pegasus.

   _____   _____

7. In many fables, wise horses give their foolish masters important warnings.

   _____   _____

DIRECTIONS ▷ **Write one sentence with each verb. Include a direct and indirect object in each one. You may use any verb tense.**

8. bring _____

   _____

9. buy _____

   _____

10. hand _____

   _____

Appositives

An **appositive** is a noun that identifies or explains the noun or pronoun it follows.
Example:
>Nguyen Luong, the *judge*, sentenced the criminal to prison.

An **appositive phrase** consists of an appositive and its modifiers.
Example:
>Nguyen Luong, *the presiding judge of the high court*, sentenced the criminal to prison.

Appositives are usually set off in commas, although sometimes dashes are used. Use commas to set off appositives that are not essential to the meaning of the sentence. Don't use commas to set off appositives when they are essential to understanding the nouns they explain.
Examples:
>The prairie, a kind of grassland, is home to many plants and animals.
>Of all my relatives, my brother Boris is the weirdest.

DIRECTIONS Underline each appositive, and insert commas where they are needed.

1. The first wedding in America the marriage of Anne Burras and John Laydon took place in 1609.

2. The first wedding broadcast on radio took place at a fair the Electrical Exposition in 1922.

3. The wedding march was played by radio station KDKA in Pittsburgh a city seven miles away.

4. My favorite strange wedding a parachute ceremony took place in 1940.

5. The participants—a minister, a bride, a groom, and four musicians—were suspended from parachutes during the ceremony.

6. John Tyler the tenth president was the first to be married while he was president.

7. His first wife Letitia had died while he held that office.

8. A "balloon wedding" a ceremony in a hot-air balloon was held in 1874 in Ohio.

9. The city of Houston site of an air show was the location of the first wedding in an airplane.

DIRECTIONS Add an appositive to each sentence. Use commas if they are needed.

10. The scorpion has a poisonous sting. _____

_____

11. Researching the subject required many hours at the library. _____

_____

12. The crowd was becoming dangerous. _____

_____

Phrases and Clauses

A **phrase** is a group of words that work together. A phrase does not have a subject or predicate. A phrase can be a prepositional, infinitive, gerund, or participial phrase.
Examples:

> *Running long distances* is no problem for me. (gerund phrase)
> The mystery of Stonehenge is a good topic *for a report*. (prepositional phrases)
> That man *kicking the soccer ball* is Pele. (participial phrase)
> Someday, I would like *to write beautiful poetry*. (infinitive phrase)

A **clause** is a group of words that has a subject and a predicate.
Example:

> The senators left the capitol *after the session was adjourned*.

DIRECTIONS ▷ Identify each underlined group of words as a *phrase* or *clause*.

1. Oprah Winfrey was born <u>on January 29, 1954</u>, in Kosciusko, Mississippi. _____

2. <u>When she was seven years old</u>, she moved to Nashville, Tennessee. _____

3. Her father encouraged her <u>to read five books</u> every two weeks. _____

4. She became the first African American woman to host a nationally distributed weekday talk show <u>on television</u>. _____

5. Her program, <u>based in Chicago</u>, went national in 1986. _____

6. <u>Besides having a successful television career</u>, Oprah has starred as a film actor. _____

7. She appeared <u>in *The Color Purple*</u> in 1985. _____

8. <u>As you know</u>, this film was based on a novel by Alice Walker. _____

DIRECTIONS ▷ Each underlined group of words is a phrase. Write *prepositional, infinitive, gerund,* or *participial* to identify each phrase.

9. <u>To have a beautiful garden</u>, you must plant, dig, weed, and rearrange constantly. _____

10. <u>Writing a best seller</u> is the goal of every novelist. _____

11. I like jogging <u>along the seashore</u> best. _____

12. Pele's first soccer ball was a stocking <u>stuffed with rags</u>. _____

13. Can you imagine steering a boat <u>without a rudder</u>? _____

14. <u>To be or not to be</u>, that is the question. _____

Independent and Dependent Clauses

A **clause** is a group of words that has a subject and a predicate.
Examples:

Indonesia <u>includes</u> more than 13,600 islands.

When <u>Indonesia won</u> its independence

An **independent clause** has a subject and predicate. It can stand alone as a sentence.
Example:

Indonesia includes more than 13,600 islands.

A **dependent clause** has a subject and predicate, but it does not express a complete thought. Therefore, it cannot stand alone as a sentence.
Example:

When Indonesia won its independence

A **subordinating conjunction** such as *until, when,* or *because* is often used to join a dependent clause and an independent clause.

DIRECTIONS Write the subject and the verb from each clause. Then, write *dependent* or *independent* on the line.

1. after the paint had been scraped away _____ _____ _____

2. fill a bucket with washing compound _____ _____ _____

3. however they continued to scrub _____ _____ _____

4. until shoulders and backs ached _____ _____ _____

5. before the painting was revealed _____ _____ _____

6. all the work was over _____ _____ _____

DIRECTIONS Write *dependent* or *independent* to identify the underlined clause. If the clause is dependent, write the subordinating conjunction that connects it with the rest of the sentence.

7. <u>Diego Rivera was one of the greatest painters and muralists of Mexico</u>.

_____

8. <u>Because he loved Mexico</u>, his works often portray the culture and history of that country.

_____

9. One of his paintings reflects the time <u>before the Spanish conquered Mexico</u>.

_____

10. <u>That painting shows the Zapotec Indians making gold jewelry</u>.

_____

Combining Dependent and Independent Clauses

Skillful writers often use subordinating conjunctions to combine related ideas. This strategy also helps writers avoid the choppy effect created by putting too many short sentences in a single paragraph. The subordinating conjunctions include words like *as, if, since, until,* and *whether.*

◎ ◎ ◎◎ ◎◎ ◎◎◎ ◎◎◎ ◎◎◎ ◎◎◎ ◎◎◎ ◎◎ ◎◎◎ ◎◎◎ ◎◎◎ ◎◎ ◎◎ ◎

DIRECTIONS ▷ **Combine the sentences using a subordinating conjunction. Write the sentence on the line.**

1. Plato was a famous philosopher. Aristotle decided to attend his school.

   _____

2. Plato died. Aristotle opened his own school to continue Plato's teachings.

   _____

3. An earthquake occurs. Tidal waves begin to form after that.

   _____

4. Find shelter. Otherwise, you will be in great danger.

   _____

5. The highest number on the Richter Scale is a 9. No earthquake has ever been recorded at that level.

   _____

   _____

6. Architects try to make their designs strong. Earthquakes can be so damaging.

   _____

7. The Richter Scale is useful. It measures the magnitude of an earthquake.

   _____

8. Pasha growled and whined. Cassie knew something was wrong.

   _____

9. Pasha paced the living room floor. He barked at Cassie.

   _____

◎◎ ◎◎ ◎◎ ◎◎◎ ◎◎ ◎◎ ◎◎ ◎◎ ◎◎ ◎◎ ◎◎ ◎◎ ◎◎ ◎◎ ◎◎◎ ◎◎

Compound Sentences

A **compound sentence** contains two or more simple sentences. The simple sentences are usually joined by a comma and a **coordinating conjunction** such as *and, but, or, for, nor, so,* or *yet*. A second way to join the simple sentences is to place a semicolon between them.

Examples:

Friction makes meteors incredibly hot, and they burn up miles above the earth's surface.

Some meteors don't burn completely; they are called meteorites.

Be careful not to confuse a compound sentence with a simple sentence that has a compound subject or compound predicate.

Examples:

Rosebud trees and magnolias bloom in the spring. (compound subject)

The three little girls whispered and pointed. (compound predicate)

◎ ◎

▌DIRECTIONS ⟩ **Read each sentence. Circle C if it is a compound sentence. Circle NC if it is not a compound.**

1. Giraffes and mice have the same number of neck bones—seven.   C   NC

2. Kiwi birds have nostrils on their beaks; they can smell earthworms underground.   C   NC

3. The pouch under a pelican's bill is huge, holding up to 25 pounds of fish.   C   NC

4. As many as 80,000 honey-producing bees can live together comfortably in one hive.   C   NC

5. Most rabbits drown in water, but the marsh rabbit can swim.   C   NC

6. Sharks have to keep moving constantly, or they suffocate.   C   NC

▌DIRECTIONS ⟩ **For each sentence, write *compound subject, compound predicate,* or *compound sentence.***

7. Armadillos are heavy, but they can inflate their stomachs with air to float on water.

   _____

8. Llamas, emus, and giraffes have unusually long necks. _____

9. The sloth eats and sleeps while hanging upside down. _____

10. Polar bears feed on seals; seals feed on fish. _____

11. Female penguins usually stay at sea, but they return when their eggs hatch.

    _____

12. Elephant mothers pick up their babies with their tusks and carry them from place to place.

    _____

Forming Compound Sentences

There are three ways to form compound sentences.
Join the two independent clauses with a coordinating conjunction (*and, but, or, nor, for, so,* and *yet*). Remember to place a comma before the conjunction.
Example:
>   Most rabbits drown in water, *but* the marsh rabbit can swim.

Insert a semicolon between the two independent clauses.
Example:
>   Polar bears feed on seals; seals feed on fish.

Connect the two independent clauses with an adverb such as *however, therefore,* or *besides*. Remember to place a semicolon before the adverb and a comma after it.
Example:
>   I'm sure I'll enjoy working with snakes; *besides,* I desperately need the money.

DIRECTIONS ⟩ **Join these independent clauses using a coordinating conjunction or a semicolon.**

1. We can wait for the package. We can leave without it.

   _____

2. I'm driving to the office in an hour. I'll pick up the supplies on the way.

   _____

3. Up went the lottery jackpot. Down went our hopes of winning.

   _____

4. Ava was ready. Her mother was not.

   _____

5. We surveyed the dirty cabin. We each shrugged silently.

   _____

DIRECTIONS ⟩ **Connect the two sentences with an adverb from the box below. Write the new sentence on the line.**

| consequently | still | further | thus | however | therefore | otherwise | **WORD BOX** |

6. We should respect our privileges. We might lose them. _____

   _____

7. Scott scrubbed hard for two hours. The walls were not ready to paint. _____

   _____

Complex Sentences

A **complex sentence** consists of one independent clause and at least one dependent clause. A **subordinating conjunction** such as *after, if,* or *when* connects the two clauses into one sentence.

Example:

> The senators left the capitol *after the session was adjourned*.

A dependent clause that begins a sentence is usually followed by a comma. If the clause ends the sentence, it usually is not preceded by a comma.

Examples:

> *Because someone was careless with matches*, a fire started at the Johnson's home.
> A fire started at the Johnson's home *because someone was careless with matches*.

When a dependent clause comes in the middle of a sentence, it is usually set off by commas.

Example:

> The fire, *which we saw spreading rapidly*, shot sparks into the sky.

DIRECTIONS ▷ Underline the dependent clause in each sentence.

1. When Lena's family made vacation plans, they chose San Francisco as their destination.

2. Because the Harrisons lived in Texas, they traveled by plane.

3. Before the plane landed, the pilot pointed out the Golden Gate Bridge.

4. Mrs. Harrison's parents have lived in San Francisco since they retired.

5. The ride took them to the top of Russian Hill, where they had a great view.

DIRECTIONS ▷ Combine the two sentences into one complex sentence, using proper punctuation to connect the ideas.

6. The Spanish founded San Francisco in 1776. They built a mission and a fort.

   _____

7. The California Gold Rush began in 1848. San Francisco grew rapidly.

   _____

8. The great earthquake and fire of 1906 destroyed much of San Francisco. The city was quickly rebuilt. _____

   _____

9. Foggy weather is common in June and July. Most people don't mind it.

   _____

10. Many visitors return to San Francisco. It is one of the most beautiful cities in America.

    _____

Avoiding Run-on Sentences

A **run-on sentence** results when two or more sentences are combined without the proper punctuation to separate them.

Example:

It was only three blocks to the restaurant we decided to walk.

A careful writer can correct run-on sentences in several ways:

Make two sentences.

If they are closely related, join the two clauses with a semicolon.

Join the two clauses with a comma and a coordinating conjunction.

Subordinate one clause to the other.

Combine ideas by using appositives and phrases.

Example:

The city council held a meeting a meeting is held every month.

The city council holds a meeting every month.

DIRECTIONS ➤ **Rewrite each run-on sentence. Use each of the ways listed at least once.**

1. The members of our city council are elected by the voters there are two thousand voters in the city.

   _____

   _____

2. There is one council member from each suburb the president is elected by the council members.

   _____

   _____

3. The current president of the council is Olivia Saenz she is the first woman to be elected to that position. _____

4. No one believed that Ms. Saenz could win her supporters began to work on her campaign.

   _____

5. The council discusses many issues every issue is decided by the full council.

   _____

6. Money is needed for many special activities the council plans fund-raisers in the city.

   _____

7. The annual city picnic is sponsored by the city council the picnic is in May.

   _____

Avoiding Wordy Language and Rambling Sentences

Careful writers use as few words as possible to relate their message. They also control sentence length so that sentences do not run on and on.

◎ ◎◎ ◎◎ ◎◎◎ ◎ ◎◎ ◎ ◎◎ ◎ ◎◎◎ ◎ ◎◎ ◎ ◎◎ ◎ ◎◎ ◎◎◎ ◎ ◎◎ ◎ ◎◎ ◎ ◎◎ ◎ ◎

DIRECTIONS ▷ **Rewrite each sentence to make it less rambling.**

1. The canoe slowly drifted down the river and I knew that we would see some really interesting wildlife beyond the bend so I was paying more attention to the riverbank than to paddling.

_____

_____

2. As we came around the bend, I nearly fell out of the canoe when I saw a large alligator sunning itself on the bank and when it saw us it slowly slipped into the water and disappeared.

_____

_____

DIRECTIONS ▷ **Underline the wordy language in each sentence.**

3. To get to Wilma's house, follow the directions that are written below for you to follow.

4. The first thing you do is get onto Highway 42 and take it to the Sun Drive exit.

5. Turn left and follow Sun Drive, which goes in a northerly direction.

6. Continue driving for four miles, and then turn left at the stop sign.

7. If you have done everything correctly and followed these directions so far, you will be on a narrow dirt road.

8. Follow this road for about 1.3 miles.

9. Look for a bright yellow ribbon tied to a tree on the left side of the road as you drive along.

10. Wilma's house is the large white house sitting right there beyond the tree, number 1120.

11. Rewrite the directions above, making them less wordy. Write the revised directions in a paragraph.

_____

_____

_____

_____

_____

_____

Capitalization

Begin every sentence and the first word of a quotation with a capital letter.
Example:
> The student exclaimed, "How can I ever get my paper done by Friday?"

Capitalize proper nouns and proper adjectives.
Example:
> Charles Dickens is my favorite author of Victorian literature.

Capitalize the first, last, and all important words in the titles of books, poems, stories, songs, and movies.
Examples:
> *The Westing Game*   "The Raven"   *Lord of the Rings*

DIRECTIONS Underline each word that should be capitalized.

1. my brother miguel plays guitar in a band.
2. The name of the band is las muchachas; its theme song is *la bamba*.
3. The lead singer, rosanna, sings some songs in spanish and some in english.
4. Last year, Mary Kate meyers found the band its first job.
5. The band played for a high school dance in cascade, washington, on valentines's day.
6. the dance was sponsored by the cascaders glee club.
7. If I finish my report for american history II, i can travel with the band next saturday.
8. Anthony said, "what time does *ghostbusters* start?"
9. francis Scott Key wrote "the star-spangled banner."
10. The book *holes* was written by texan louis sachar in 1998.
11. The librarian stated, "that book won the newbery medal in 1999."
12. It was published by Farrar, straus & giroux, which is based in New York city.

DIRECTIONS Write a sentence to show these uses of capital letters.

13. name of a restaurant in your community _____

_____

14. a direct quotation _____

_____

15. name of a college or university _____

_____

16. name of a country _____

More About Capitalization

Capitalize a personal title when it precedes a person's name. Also capitalize the abbreviation of the title.
Examples:

Governor Shelton   Ms. Piercy   Justice Marshall   Dr. Garza

Capitalize the names of days and months, along with their abbreviations.
Examples:

Saturday   Sat.   December   Dec.

Capitalize abbreviations used in addresses. Capitalize both letters in the abbreviations of state names.
Examples:

St.   Ave.   Blvd.   CA   TX   FL

DIRECTIONS Rewrite each sentence using correct capitalization.

1. "the bravest people in the world are Doctors," rani said.

2. She continued, "my Stepsister indira has been working in calcutta since march."

3. "Does she work at mercy major hospital," Ben asked, "Or at Calcutta general?"

4. "Actually, indira is a Specialist in internal medicine at the Clinic on empire street," answered Rani.

5. "Indira once worked with mother Theresa," Rani finished proudly, "The famous albanian nun."

DIRECTIONS Underline each word and abbreviation that should be capitalized.

6. silvas high school science fair
   thur., nov. 10th, 9 A.M.
   328 n. canyon blvd.

7. danton water festival
   july 19–21
   brighton dam
   lakeview, mn 67104

8. jeannette duran
   347 antero st.
   markham, ontario L3R 1ES

9. capt. c. j. hatori
   c/o ocean star
   p.o. box 5523
   gateway, nh 07621

Plural Nouns

A **plural noun** names more than one person, place, thing, or idea. Most plural nouns are formed by adding *s* or *es* to the singular form. There are, however, many exceptions to this rule.

Examples:

       word—words   watch—watch*es*   party—par*ties*   shelf—shel*ves*

A few nouns have **irregular plural** forms. Some even keep the same form for both singular and plural.

Examples:

       child—*children*   trout—*trout*

DIRECTIONS ▷ **Write the plural form of the nouns in parentheses on the lines.**

1. (wish) In a game my family plays, we each have three _____.

2. (safe) My practical sister always wants three _____ filled with money.

3. (tax) Once, she also asked for one million dollars with no _____.

4. (hero) I always ask to meet all my _____.

5. (peach) Juan, who enjoys desserts, asked for a basket of _____.

6. (kiss) My baby sister asked for 100 hugs and _____.

7. (key) Creativity is one of the _____ to being a good wish-maker.

8. (personality) What people wish for tells a great deal about their _____.

9. (vacation) Mama sometimes wishes for separate _____ for her and her children.

10. (woman) My guess is that many _____ silently wish for the same thing.

DIRECTIONS ▷ **Circle the correct plural noun and use it in a sentence.**

11. deers   deer   deerses

_____

12. handfuls   handsful   handsfuls

_____

13. oxes   oxs   oxen

_____

14. mother-in-laws   mothers-in-law

_____

Possessive Nouns

A **possessive noun** shows ownership or possession. An **apostrophe (')** is used to form a possessive noun. To form the possessive of most **singular nouns**, add an apostrophe and *s*.
Examples:

the symphonies *of Beethoven* = *Beethoven's* symphonies
the lead singer *of the band* = the *band's* lead singer

To form the possessive of a **plural noun** that does not end in *s*, add an apostrophe and *s*. If the plural noun does end in *s*, add only an apostrophe.
Examples:

the escape route *of the mice* = the *mice's* escape route
the courage *of the citizens* = the *citizens'* courage

DIRECTIONS ▸ Identify which groups of words in these sentences could be replaced with possessive nouns. Then, rewrite each sentence.

1. The feet of a hummingbird are so weak that the bird never walks. _____

_____

2. The feet of hyraxes form suction cups to climb trees. _____

_____

3. The feet of a sloth are specialized for hanging in trees. _____

_____

4. The forefeet of giraffes are used for kicking predators. _____

_____

5. The body of a centipede can have 95 pairs of legs. _____

_____

6. The paws of pandas have "thumbs" that help them grasp bamboo shoots. _____

_____

DIRECTIONS ▸ Write the plural form of each noun. Then, write the possessive form of the plural noun.

7. goose _____   _____

8. wolf _____   _____

9. spy _____   _____

10. ox _____   _____

Commas

As with all punctuation marks, **commas** helps writers clarify their meaning and prevent confusion.

Examples:

> To be successful firefighters must continue to study new methods of first aid.
> (unclear)
>
> To be successful, firefighters must continue to study new methods of first aid.
> (clear)

Rules about comma use are numerous. Here are a few.

Use a comma after a word or phrase that introduces a sentence.

Use a comma to set off the name or title of a person who is spoken to directly.

Use commas to set off words or phrases that interrupt the flow of the sentence.

Use commas to set off nonrestrictive appositives.

Use a comma after each item in a series.

DIRECTIONS ▷ **Correct each sentence by inserting commas where necessary.**

1. My favorite instrument the trumpet has a long history.

2. Trumpets in fact are at least 3,500 years old.

3. Silver and bronze trumpets were found in the tomb of Tutankhamen the boy pharaoh of ancient Egypt.

4. In the opinion of many experts these trumpets were used for royal ceremonies.

5. Originally however trumpets could sound only one or two notes.

6. Bones canes reeds and shells were hollowed out to make trumpets.

7. By 1400 though the straight trumpet was bent into an S-shape.

8. Later I've read it became a single-form loop.

9. According to the encyclopedia valves came into use only in the nineteenth century.

10. I asked Mr. Ortega our band leader about the trumpet.

11. "Mr. Ortega when did you learn to play the trumpet?"

12. "My uncle a fine trumpet player taught me when I was only ten years old."

13. "Who are your favorite trumpeters sir?"

14. "Perry the greatest masters of the trumpet are Louis Armstrong Dizzy Gillespie and Miles Davis."

15. "You know Perry some jazz trumpeters also play classical music."

16. "Wynton Marsalis for example is a fine classical musician."

Commas in Compound and Complex Sentences

A compound sentence contains two or more simple sentences that are connected by a coordinating conjunction such as *and, but, or, for, nor, yet,* and *so.* Place a **comma** in front of the conjunction to punctuate the sentence correctly.
Example:
> Some dinosaurs of the Mesozoic Era were ferocious, *but* others were peaceful.

A complex sentence contains one independent clause and at least one dependent clause. If the dependent clause comes at the beginning or middle of a sentence, use **commas** to separate it from the rest of the sentence.
Examples:
> *Although Plateosaurus was huge,* other reptiles were much more savage.
> Other reptiles, *which were smaller than the huge Plateosaurus,* were quite savage.

DIRECTIONS Correct each sentence by inserting commas where necessary.

1. The salmon was the most endangered animal of the 1990s so it is worth studying.

2. Logging caused a problem for the spotted owl but the causes of the salmon problem are more complex.

3. Because a number of species of salmon are threatened solutions will cost a great deal.

4. Where salmon spawn each year in the upper Columbia River Basin the fish used to number about 12 million.

5. That number which is now down to about 2,500,000 may decrease further.

6. As some scientists calculate perhaps nineteen types of salmon may already be extinct.

7. Irrigation runoff water contains dangerous chemicals and dams have reduced the water flow to rivers.

8. These two factors have damaged the rivers of the Northwest but overfishing and building developments have also contributed.

9. Because dams block the water flow the young salmon are not carried out to sea on strong currents of fresh water.

10. Because a seven-year drought has also decreased the fresh water even more fish have died.

11. Fish born in man-made hatcheries lack the energy of wild salmon so they do not swim upstream well.

12. Before real help for the salmon is possible emergency rulings from the government may be necessary.

Semicolons

Use a **semicolon (;)** to join independent clauses if they are not joined by *and, but , for, nor, or, so,* or *yet.*
Example:

> The hurricane lashed the house with gale-force winds; we were scared out of our wits.

Use a semicolon between clauses of a compound sentence that are joined by connecting words such as *therefore, however, thus,* and *then.*
Example:

> Citizens were warned to evacuate the area; nevertheless, we refused to leave.

DIRECTIONS > Rewrite these sentences, adding semicolons where necessary.

1. Caring for a pet is a big responsibility it takes a lot of time and effort. _____

_____

2. My dog Homer is my best friend however I get angry with him occasionally. _____

_____

3. Homer is like all dogs he can be a pest sometimes. _____

_____

4. A cat fell from a boat into the lake Homer jumped right in after it. _____

_____

5. Homer can be noisy, dirty, and disobedient still he is irresistible. _____

_____

DIRECTIONS > Write your own sentences using the connecting word given. Use semicolons correctly.

6. however _____

_____

7. therefore _____

_____

8. nevertheless _____

_____

Colons, Dashes, and Parentheses

Use a **colon (:)** to introduce a series and to separate hours and minutes when expressing time. A colon is also placed after the greeting in a business letter.
Example:

> The student brought three things to class: the textbook, adequate writing materials, and a willingness to learn.

Use a **dash (—)** to mark a sudden change or break in thought or speech.
Example:

> The shelter—made of branches, vegetation, and palm strips—was barely adequate for survival.

Use **parentheses ( )** around words or phrases that break into the main thought of a sentence but are not of major importance.
Example:

> Italian astronomer Gallileo (1564–1642) was detained and questioned during the Spanish Inquisition.

DIRECTIONS ▷ **Rewrite these sentences, adding colons, parentheses, and dashes where necessary.**

1. Animals need care in the following areas shelter, food, exercise, and grooming.

_____

2. I am responsible for these chores feeding the dog, walking him, and sweeping up the dog hair.

_____

3. I have to walk our dog, Homer, at 630 every morning.

_____

4. Sometimes Homer watch out can be very destructive.

_____

5. Our previous dog, Cuthbert 1985–2000, was not nearly as accident-prone as Homer is.

_____

6. Of course, Cuthbert was a different kind of dog about 80 pounds worth of different!

_____

7. Another curious thing Homer is very fond of our vet.

_____

8. He's quite enthusiastic a maniac at the vet's office.

_____

9. Yesterday you won't believe this Homer saved a drowning cat.

_____

Titles of Documents

Capitalize the first word, last word, and all important words in a title.
Put quotation marks around the titles of short works, such as poems, short stories, chapters of books, articles, and songs.
Examples:

"The Road Not Taken," "Rock Steady," "The Tell-Tale Heart"
Underline the titles of books, plays, magazines, newspapers, television shows, and movies. If you are using a computer to write, replace underlining with italics.
Examples:

People, The Chicago Tribune, Sounder   *People, The Chicago Tribune, Sounder*

DIRECTIONS ▷ **Rewrite the sentences, adding capital letters, quotation marks, and underlines where they are needed.**

1. In English class this year, we studied Lois Lowry's the giver.

   _____

2. In the library, Gil found a copy of Laurence Yep's dragon's gate.

   _____

3. Kara liked Langston Hughes's poem long trip.

   _____

4. Maria's favorite short story was after twenty years by O. Henry.

   _____

5. The story machine is a play by Isaac Asimov.

   _____

6. I like the magazine newsweek.

   _____

DIRECTIONS ▷ **Read each title, noting the kind of work it is. Rewrite each title correctly.**

7. it's a wonderful life (movie) _____

8. a young style for an old story (newspaper article) _____

9. getting to know you (song) _____

10. the song of the moon (poem) _____

11. pacific crossing (book) _____

12. i love lucy (television show) _____

13. a forest in the clouds (book chapter) _____

Direct Quotations and Dialogue

Use quotation marks before and after the exact words of a speaker.
Example:
"The truth is powerful and will prevail," said Sojourner Truth.
If a quote is interrupted by other words, place the quotation marks around the quoted words only. Use a comma to separate the quotation from the rest of the sentence.
Example:
"Give me liberty," cried Patrick Henry, "or give me death!"
Place a question mark or an exclamation point inside closing quotation marks only if the quotation itself is a question or an exclamation.
Example:
"Haven't you ever heard of Sojourner Truth or Patrick Henry?" asked Marcia.

DIRECTIONS Rewrite these sentences, inserting correct capitalization, punctuation, and quotation marks.

1. Queen Elizabeth I ruled a great empire, said Marcia.

2. She told her critics, I have the heart and stomach of a king.

3. Who else had a great impact on a country? asked Terri.

4. Well, Ben remarked, Mohandas Gandhi inspired a nonviolent revolution in India.

5. Write the dialogue correctly. Remember to start a new paragraph each time the speaker changes.

Teach me how to play chess said Devon. What are these eight small pieces called he questioned. Those pieces, Sarah answered, are called pawns. They are the weakest pieces on the chessboard. How about the queen asked Devon. Now the queen is a different story. She can move in any direction until her path is blocked Sarah explained. So Devon reasoned if your queen is captured, I guess you're in real trouble. Not necessarily Sarah replied. I've won games with only two bishops and a rook.

Continue on your own paper.

Abbreviations, Acronyms, and Initialisms

An **abbreviation** is a short way of writing something. Common abbreviations include those for units of measure (*doz, Hz, in., lb*), personal titles (*Dr., Capt., Ms.*), dates and times (*A.M., Oct., Mon.*), and postal terms (*TX, St., CA, Ave.*).

An **acronym** is a kind of abbreviation. Acronyms are formed from the first letters of a series of words, and they always create a pronounceable word. **Initialisms** are similar to acronyms because they are also formed from the first letters of a series of words. Initialisms are *not*, however, pronounced as a word.

Acronyms: *RAM* (random access memory)
           NASA (National Aeronautics and Space Administration)

Initialisms: PTA (Parent Teacher Association)   USA (United States of America)

DIRECTIONS ▷ Write the abbreviation of each term. Use a dictionary if necessary.

1. Fahrenheit _____

2. New Mexico _____

3. 2.5 milliliters _____

4. Governor Smith _____

5. National Basketball Association _____

6. miles per hour _____

7. Central Intelligence Agency _____

8. Incorporated _____

DIRECTIONS ▷ The underlined abbreviations would be more appropriately written out since each is a part of a sentence. On the lines, write the word or words that were abbreviated.

9. I read an article about sharks in the <u>Sept.</u> issue of a science magazine. _____

10. The largest shark in the ocean, the white shark, measures up to 49 <u>ft</u> in length. _____

11. The smallest shark measures only 15–20 <u>cm</u> in length. _____

12. Some of my friends have seen sharks off the coast of <u>FL</u>. _____

DIRECTIONS ▷ Write out the words that the abbreviations stand for. Then, write *acronym* or *initialism* to identify the kind of abbreviation.

13. FBI _____

14. scuba _____

15. U.N. _____

16. ROM _____

Contractions

Form **contractions** by joining two words together and replacing one or more letters with an apostrophe.
Examples:

        is not = isn't   they will = they'll   who is (or who has) = who's

Be careful when you write sentences that contain contractions formed with the word *not* (*can't, won't, didn't*). These contractions are negatives, so you must avoid putting another negative word in the same sentence.
Examples:

        Nobody can't tell the twins apart. (double negative—incorrect)
        Nobody can tell the twins apart. (correct)

◎ ◎◎ ◎◎ ◎◎◎ ◎◎ ◎◎ ◎ ◎◎ ◎ ◎◎ ◎◎ ◎◎ ◎◎ ◎◎◎ ◎◎ ◎◎ ◎◎ ◎◎ ◎

DIRECTIONS ▷ **Rewrite each sentence, using the correct contraction.**

1. Are you not the novelist who wrote this book?

   _____

2. In my opinion, the photo on your book's jacket will not be any advantage to you.

   _____

3. Why can new novelists not have some common sense?

   _____

4. Perhaps you can take advice from someone who has got experience.

   _____

5. You will be sorry for putting a grinning photo on your book.

   _____

6. I have got only one author photo on my shelf—this one of myself.

   _____

7. I am not grinning in that photo.

   _____

8. I had just had the flu the week before the photo was taken.

   _____

DIRECTIONS ▷ **Write the contraction for each pair of words.**

9. did not _____

10. will not _____

11. she is _____

12. who is _____

13. does not _____

14. she has _____

Prefixes and Suffixes

A **prefix** is a word part that is added to the beginning of a base word. Prefixes change the meaning of base words.
Examples:

    *dis*appear   *in*definite   *mis*manage   *re*arrange

A **suffix** is a word part that is added to the end of a base word. Suffixes also change the meaning of base words.
Examples:

    worth*less*   kind*ness*   break*able*   educat*ion*

Some words have both a prefix and suffix.
Examples:

    *un*forgett*able*   *im*possibil*ity*   *dis*respect*ful*   *re*creat*ion*

▷ **DIRECTIONS**   **Examine the parts of each underlined word to figure out its meaning. Fill in the blanks correctly, and write a definition of the word.**

1. The exhausted surgeon dreaded telling the patient's family that John has an <u>incurable</u> disease.

   The prefix _____ means "not," and the suffix _____ means

   "able to." The definition of *incurable* is _____.

2. The armadillo is a <u>prehistoric</u> creature with distinctive armor but an underdeveloped brain.

   The prefix _____ means "before," and the suffix _____

   means "relating to." The definition of *prehistoric* is _____.

3. After hiding my slippers and shredding the newspaper, my <u>unrepentant</u> puppy wagged his tail and

   fell asleep.

   The prefix _____ means "not," and the suffix _____ means

   "inclined to." The definition of *unrepentant* is _____.

4. Many environmental groups are concerned about the <u>deforestation</u> of Central America.

   The prefix _____ means "down" or "away," and the suffix

   _____ means "the act of." The definition of *deforestation* is

   _____.

5. The <u>coexistence</u> of cowbirds and livestock illustrates how mammals adapt to one another in nature.

   The prefix _____ means "together," and the suffix _____

   means "the act of." The definition of *coexistence* is _____.

More About Prefixes and Suffixes

A **prefix** is a word part that is added to the beginning of a base word. Prefixes change the meaning of base words.

Examples:

       *dis*appear   *in*definite   *mis*manage   *re*arrange

A **suffix** is a word part that is added to the end of a base word. Suffixes also change the meaning of base words.

Examples:

       worth*less*   kind*ness*   break*able*   educat*ion*

Some words have both a prefix and suffix.

Examples:

       *un*forget*table*   *im*possibi*lity*   *dis*respect*ful*   *re*creat*ion*

DIRECTIONS — Underline each word in the paragraph that has both a prefix and a suffix.

After the peak of the gold rush in America, many towns became suddenly depopulated. Conflicts arose because some people became rich while others struggled to survive. Many friendships suffered irreparable damage. After a while, new gold strikes became infrequent, and disheartened prospectors left to start a new way of life. Still others became disenchanted with the inhospitable climate or the unrefined nature of town life. Life in a gold-rush town was unpredictable, even at times unmanageable. It is indisputable that a person would need to have a strong spirit of adventure to survive for any length of time in a gold-rush town.

DIRECTIONS — Write the words you underlined in the paragraph. Then, write their definitions. Use a dictionary if necessary.

      Word   **Meaning**

1. _____   _____

2. _____   _____

3. _____   _____

4. _____   _____

5. _____   _____

6. _____   _____

7. _____   _____

8. _____   _____

9. _____   _____

Compounds, Blends, and Clipped Words

A **compound word** is made up of two smaller words. **Open compounds** are written as separate words; **closed compounds** are written as one word. **Hyphenated compounds** have hyphens between the smaller words.
Examples:
    post office   newspaper   baby-sitter
A **blend** is a combination of parts of words into one word.
Examples:
    swipe (sweep + wipe)   slang (slovenly + language)   Medicare (medicine + care)
A **clipped word** is a shortened version of a longer word.
Examples:
    limo (limosine)   max (maximum)   demo (demonstration)

DIRECTIONS Underline the compounds, blends, and clipped words in the paragraph. Label the compound words *CP*, the blends *BL,* and the clipped words *CL*.

Homecoming weekend for the alums of Madison Prep was an outstanding success. Previous classmates, now meeting as grown-ups, held their reunion in the ivied hallways that their forebears had used for generations. Since most alums arrived at the dorms late and slept in, the first event of the day was brunch. The chair of the event had asked the servers to dress in the navy-and-white uniforms the alums had worn when they attended prep school. The women, some with their hair in ponytails, gossiped about old boyfriends. Meanwhile, the old baseball team took on the basketball team in a fierce Hearts tournament. In the late afternoon, when farewells were said, more than a few tears glittered on smiling faces.

DIRECTIONS Write the correct blend on the lines.

1. motor + hotel = _____   7. smoke + fog = _____

2. splash + spatter = _____   8. fourteen + nights = _____

3. flame + glare = _____   9. sky + laboratory = _____

4. international + network = _____   10. parachute + troops = _____

5. marionette + puppet = _____   11. dance + exercise = _____

6. prim + sissy = _____   12. network + etiquette = _____

Synonyms

Synonyms are words that have similar meanings.
Examples:

        tale, story, myth, legend, fantasy, parable, yarn

◎◎◎ ◎◎ ◎◎ ◎◎◎ ◎◎ ◎◎ ◎◎◎ ◎◎ ◎◎ ◎◎◎ ◎◎ ◎◎ ◎◎ ◎◎ ◎

DIRECTIONS ▷ **Write one synonym for the underlined word in each sentence.**

1. As a child, did you ever play with a <u>strange</u> molding material? _____

2. Who came up with the idea to <u>make</u> some gooey stuff for children to mold? _____

3. The answer is that <u>nobody</u> did! _____

4. In the early 1940s, U.S. companies were searching for a <u>cheap</u> substitute for rubber. _____

5. An engineer named James Wright succeeded in creating <u>fake</u> rubber. _____

6. It could <u>stretch</u> more than rubber did. _____

7. Molds and decay did not <u>harm</u> it, and it bounced 25 percent higher than a real

rubber ball. _____

8. Unfortunately, this new "stuff," while <u>interesting</u>, had no real practical advantages over rubber.

_____

9. Employees at the lab called the <u>new</u> stuff "nutty putty" and showed it to people who came to visit.

_____

DIRECTIONS ▷ **Read the paragraph. Write a synonym for each underlined word in the space provided.**

    Marcus was (10) <u>afraid</u> of tarantulas. He didn't care that people (11) <u>said</u> tarantulas were actually harmless. He was (12) <u>repulsed</u> by the thought of their huge, hairy bodies. Marcus had heard that in Texas they crawled along walls and (13) <u>hung</u> from ceilings. Having this (14) <u>information</u> was enough to make Marcus's skin crawl.

10. _____

11. _____

12. _____

13. _____

14. _____

Antonyms

Antonyms are words that have opposite meanings.
Examples:

adult—child   start—stop   fresh—stale   quickly—slowly

DIRECTIONS ▷ **Write two antonyms for each word.**

1. arrive _____ _____

2. tired _____ _____

3. fantastic _____ _____

4. dishonesty _____ _____

5. quickly _____ _____

6. friend _____ _____

7. boring _____ _____

8. conceal _____ _____

9. turbulent _____ _____

10. difficult _____ _____

11. fortunate _____ _____

12. advance _____ _____

DIRECTIONS ▷ **Write one synonym and one antonym for each word.**

Word	Synonym	Antonym
13. demonstrate	_____	_____
14. appreciate	_____	_____
15. leader	_____	_____
16. confident	_____	_____
17. establish	_____	_____
18. frequent	_____	_____
19. afraid	_____	_____
20. buy	_____	_____
21. modern	_____	_____

Homographs—Words with Multiple Meanings

> **Homographs** are words that are spelled the same but have different meanings. They are often pronounced differently.
> *Example:*
> The *invalid* has been in the hospital for three months.
> The test has become *invalid* because the standards are different this year.

◎ ◎◎ ◎◎◎ ◎◎◎◎◎ ◎◎ ◎◎ ◎◎◎◎◎◎ ◎◎ ◎◎◎ ◎◎◎ ◎◎ ◎◎◎ ◎◎ ◎◎ ◎

DIRECTIONS ➤ **Underline the homograph in each sentence. Write both meanings of the word on the line.**

1. From studying the minute patterns in a leaf to hiking along beautiful trails, I enjoyed every minute of the camping trip. _____

2. After reviewing the content of my rough draft, my tutor was content with the quality of my paper.
_____

3. Soldiers who are based in the desert rarely desert their posts because they have no place to go.
_____

4. The high lead content in paints can lead to serious health problems for those who work with it.
_____

5. The EMS worker wound a clean, cotton bandage around the victim's chest wound.
_____

6. The protesters refuse to leave until the council hears their resolution about the correct disposal of refuse. _____

7. When the rainstorm began, I dove for cover, and the little dove disappeared into the underbrush.
_____

8. Advocates of the homeless object to their clients' being treated as objects of scorn.
_____

DIRECTIONS ➤ **Write the homograph for each pair of meanings below.**

_____ **9.** a. to delay	b. a place for horses
_____ **10.** a. to ease grief	b. a cabinet
_____ **11.** a. to turn	b. air in motion
_____ **12.** a. to become weary	b. the rubber around a wheel

◎ ◎◎◎◎◎ ◎◎◎ ◎◎ ◎◎◎ ◎◎◎◎◎ ◎◎ ◎◎◎ ◎◎◎◎◎◎ ◎◎◎ ◎◎◎ ◎◎◎ ◎◎

Homophones

Homophones are words that sound alike but have different meanings and different spellings.

Example:

The recordings of that new grunge *band* were *banned* in the United States.

◎ ◎◎ ◎◎ ◎ ◎◎◎◎◎ ◎◎ ◎◎ ◎◎◎ ◎◎◎◎ ◎◎◎◎ ◎◎◎ ◎◎ ◎◎◎ ◎◎ ◎◎ ◎ ◎

▌ DIRECTIONS ▷ **Underline the homophone pair in each sentence.**

1. Dad said, "Pack up the tents! I've been feeling tense lately, so we're going camping."

2. I didn't know where we were going, but I knew I had nothing to wear on a camping expedition.

3. Not knowing when the stores would close, I hurried to the mall to look for appropriate clothes.

4. Those days of hiking and swimming and camping went by in a beautiful daze.

▌ DIRECTIONS ▷ **Underline the correct homophones in the sentences.**

5. The night (air, heir) is (sew, so) cool that you will (knead, need) a light jacket.

6. The small plants were set out in orderly (rows, rose).

7. Lee (seams, seems) to have forgotten about (our, hour) plans for the picnic.

8. I (knew, new) those (knew, new) shoes would hurt my (feat, feet).

9. We did (not, knot) go to the (seen, scene) of the wreck.

10. If this diet succeeds, I (mite, might) be able to fasten this belt around my (waist, waste).

▌ DIRECTIONS ▷ **Write the homophone for each word listed below.**

11. peace _____	19. altar _____
12. principle _____	20. meet _____
13. boarder _____	21. sight _____
14. billed _____	22. cent _____
15. pause _____	23. way _____
16. sum _____	24. guessed _____
17. bawl _____	25. ate _____
18. him _____	26. blew _____

◎◎◎ ◎◎◎ ◎◎ ◎◎◎◎◎ ◎◎ ◎◎ ◎◎◎ ◎◎◎◎ ◎◎◎◎ ◎◎◎ ◎◎ ◎◎◎ ◎◎ ◎

Denotation and Connotation

The **denotation** of a word is its exact meaning as stated in a dictionary.
The **connotation** of a word is the feeling that a word suggests when it is used. Some words are neutral in connotation; others carry a suggestion that something is positive or negative.
Examples:

house (neutral)   home (positive)   hovel (negative)

DIRECTIONS ▷ Use the pairs of words to complete the sentences. Then, write *positive, negative,* or *neutral* to indicate the connotation of the word.

left   abandoned

1. Before going on vacation, the owners _____ the puppy at the vet's.

   _____

2. Before going on vacation, the owners _____ the puppy at the vet's.

   _____

gaudy   ornate

3. The _____ carvings that decorated the mantel made a dramatic impression.

   _____

4. The _____ carvings that decorated the mantel made a dramatic impression.

   _____

paintings   masterpieces

5. The *Mona Lisa*, which hangs in the Louvre, is one of Leonardo da Vinci's

   _____ . _____

6. The *Mona Lisa*, which hangs in the Louvre, is one of Leonardo da Vinci's

   _____ . _____

loud   enthusiastic

7. A group of _____ regulars eats at Arno's every Friday night.

   _____

8. A group of _____ regulars eats at Arno's every Friday night.

   _____

Idioms

An **idiom** is a group of words that has a different meaning from the literal definition of its parts. Idioms are often colorful expressions used in speech and in informal writing, but they should be used carefully in formal writing.
Examples:

> People can *get into hot water* when they speak before they think. (idiom)
> People can *make serious mistakes* when they speak before they think.
> (better sentence)

DIRECTIONS Underline the idiom in each sentence. Rewrite the sentence, substituting other words in place of the underlined idioms. Make any changes necessary.

1. For our English assignment, we are to list all the idioms we come across as we read.

   _____

2. Because I have spoken English for only three years, understanding idioms is hardly a piece of cake for me. _____

   _____

3. Nevertheless, I have come a long way in the past three years.

   _____

4. Marta thinks works of modern fiction are the best bet for finding idioms.

   _____

5. Because I need to make a good grade, I'm going to take my time finishing the assignment.

   _____

6. Marta says I will get the hang of it if I concentrate on the exact meaning of each word.

   _____

7. Fortunately, my tutor is willing to bend over backwards to help me improve my English.

   _____

8. In the long run, studying idioms will help me to better understand my new language.

   _____

9. It is little consolation to know that all the Vietnamese students are in the same boat.

   _____

10. We are working diligently to make the most of our new lives in Ontario.

   _____

Clichés

A **cliché** is a word or phrase that has become overused and, therefore, no longer communicates effectively. Clichés come to mind easily because they are familiar. However, they are usually wordy and vague. Clichés should be used sparingly in formal writing.

Example:

Run it up the flagpole. (cliché)

See what others think. (better expression of idea)

DIRECTIONS Underline the clichés in each sentence. Rewrite the sentences as much as is necessary to express the ideas more precisely.

1. In business, profit is always the bottom line.

_____

2. The estimated cost of adding to the product line is a ballpark figure.

_____

3. Since this is the final year of the project, let's go out in a blaze of glory.

_____

4. The true identity of Watergate's "Deep Throat" will never see the light of day.

_____

5. The customer rejected the sketches, so the architects are back to square one.

_____

6. These are the winning lottery numbers, beyond a shadow of a doubt.

_____

7. Production will grind to a halt if the rumored layoffs occur.

_____

8. The university's new computer system provides state-of-the-art technology.

_____

9. Using nonstandard English is a definite no-no.

_____

10. The new RV by Edsel has passed the acid test of automotive design.

_____

Figurative Language

Figurative language, such as similes and metaphors, can add information and clarify meaning in new and creative ways. A **simile** compares two unlike things using the words *like* or *as*. A **metaphor** compares two unlike things without using the words *like* or *as*.

Examples:

Above, the stars were *as bright as headlights*. (simile)

Above, the stars were *headlights, guiding our steps*. (metaphor)

DIRECTIONS Complete each sentence using descriptive vocabulary. Circle *S* if the sentence is a simile or *M* if it is a metaphor.

1. S M The old book was as dusty as _____

_____

2. S M The poem about the homeless was a _____

_____

3. S M The people snorted and stomped in the snow like _____

_____

4. S M A boat slipped by in the fog like _____

_____

5. S M On the dark highway, the toll booth was a _____

_____

6. S M In my imagination, the foreign land was a _____

_____

7. S M With her nose buried in a book, she looked like _____

_____

8. S M When he unwrapped the new book, his face lit up like _____

_____

9. S M The chariot was a _____

_____

10. S M The horn of the freighter cut through the night like _____

_____

Subject-Verb Agreement

A subject and verb must agree in number. Use the singular form of a verb with a singular subject and the plural form with a plural subject. Remember that most collective and mass nouns take a singular verb.
Example:

A large *crowd* is expected.   The *grass* is growing rapidly.

Sometimes a prepositional phrase lies between the subject and verb. Remember that the verb must agree with the sentence's subject, not with the object of the preposition.
Example:

The *colors* in the painting *are* vivid.

A compound subject joined by *and* requires a plural verb. When a compound subject is joined by *or* or *nor*, the verb must agree with the subject closest to the verb.
Example:

The student or her *parents are required* to sign the release form.

DIRECTIONS ▷ **Write the correct verb on the line.**

1. (is, are) Hard work and a good attitude _____ important to us.

2. (is, are) The good news _____ our winning record.

3. (give, gives) Headlines usually _____ credit to a particular goal or save.

4. (is, are) Teamwork _____ really the winner.

5. (deserve, deserves) The pep squad _____ some of the credit, too.

6. (understand, understands) Each of us _____ team spirit.

7. (work, works) We all _____ together.

DIRECTIONS ▷ **Write a predicate to complete each sentence. Use a verb in the present tense.**

8. The coaches at our school _____

9. My soccer coach _____

10. The soccer team _____

11. The crowd _____

12. Neither the players nor the coach _____

13. The team uniforms _____

14. The season _____

15. Most of the equipment _____

Avoiding Double Negatives

Nonstandard English is always wrong for the writing you do in school unless you are creating dialogue. Using double negatives is nonstandard English and must be avoided.
A **negative** is word that means "no" or "not." Contractions that end in *n't* are negatives.
Examples:

> never, no one, neither, barely, hardly, don't, won't, can't

A **double negative** occurs when a writer puts two or more negative words in the same sentence.
Example:

> *No one* should *never* drive on ice. (double negative)
> No one should ever drive on ice. (correct English)

DIRECTIONS ▷ **Underline the negatives in each sentence. Rewrite sentences that contain a double negative. Write *correct* if the sentence does not contain a double negative.**

1. Hardly nobody knows about the mummy the Russians found in Siberia.

_____

2. Gold prospectors hadn't barely begun digging when they found something strange.

_____

3. No one had never seen nothing like it.

_____

4. Nothing like this creature existed except in ancient cave drawings.

_____

5. Scientists couldn't scarcely believe it—it was a baby mammoth!

_____

6. Mammoths hadn't existed on Earth for at least 9,000 years.

_____

7. Although this mammoth was very young when it died, it wasn't no tiny creature.

_____

_____

8. The prospectors couldn't hardly get the mummy out of the ground.

_____

9. Another mummy won't be found nowhere around there until summer.

_____

10. The ground in Siberia doesn't never thaw out until then.

_____

Avoiding Nonstandard Verb Forms

Nonstandard English is always wrong for the writing you do in school unless you are creating dialogue. Certain forms of verbs are mistakenly used as correct but are actually nonstandard forms of the verb.
Examples:

> ain't, growed, throwed

Never use nonstandard verbs. They are incorrect.

DIRECTIONS ▷ **Underline the nonstandard verbs. Rewrite the sentences.**

1. Our people need health benefits, and we ain't about to take no for an answer.

_____

2. The test wasn't as difficult as I expected, but nobody knowed the answer to the bonus question.

_____

_____

3. "Why, look at those kids. They're all growed up!" said Great Aunt Matilda.

_____

4. At the last World Series, the President throwed out the first ball.

_____

5. Frank fell out of the tree and busted his arm.

_____

6. The blind date should have been successful, but the guy brung along his dog!

_____

7. Raymond, who really needed a new bike, couldn't believe a 6-year-old drawed the winning raffle

ticket. _____

_____

8. He heared the little girl's feet couldn't even touch the pedals.

_____

9. Hurricanes nearly drownded half of Louisiana this season.

_____

10. The gale-force winds blowed at nearly 70 miles per hour.

_____

Pronoun-Antecedent Agreement

An **antecedent** is the noun or nouns to which a pronoun refers. A pronoun should agree with its antecedent in number and gender.
Examples:

> In 1847, *Homan Walsh* offered *his* help to some railway engineers. The *engineers* were building a suspension bridge at Niagara Falls, and *they* were having trouble. Antecedents are often in the same sentence with their pronouns. Sometimes, however, the antecedent is in another sentence.

Example:

> Heavy *cables* crossed a steep gorge. How to get *them* across the gorge was the problem.

◎ ◎

DIRECTIONS ▷ **Underline each pronoun, and write its antecedent on the line.**

1. As president of the Senate in the 1830s, Martin Van Buren kept a gun near him to maintain order.

   _____

2. During the Civil War, Emma Edmonds spied for the Union after disguising herself as a male slave.

   _____

3. Dr. Mary Walker, a surgeon, tended Union soldiers and spent time with them in a Confederate prison.

   _____

4. "The Battle Hymn of the Republic" was a popular song with Union soldiers as they fought in the Civil War.

   _____

5. Julia Ward Howe's song was published in a magazine, but she was not named as the author.

   _____

6. Howe, along with her husband Samuel, was the editor of the *Boston Commonwealth*.

   _____

7. Many famous poets of the day voiced their praise for the inspiring lyrics of the song.

   _____

8. Howe's words have remained popular with soldiers, who sang the same song during World War I.

   _____

DIRECTIONS ▷ **Write the pronoun that is needed to complete each sentence.**

9. Anna Taylor went to Niagara Falls, but _____ crossed them in a very unusual way.

10. Witnesses watched with _____ mouths open.

11. Anna Taylor had squeezed _____ into a barrel.

12. Was Taylor the first person to survive a trip over Niagara Falls? Of course _____ was!

◎ ◎

Active Voice and Passive Voice

When a sentence is written in **active voice**, the subject of the sentence performs the action described in the sentence. **Passive voice** means that the subject of the sentence receives the action described in the sentence.
Examples:

The *members* of the drill team washed the cars. (active voice)
The subject (*members*) is **performing** the washing.
The *cars* were washed by the members of the drill team. (passive voice)
The subject (*cars*) is **receiving** the action.

DIRECTIONS ▷ **Identify each underlined verb as active or passive. Write *A* if the verb is in active voice, *P* if it is in passive voice. Then rewrite each sentence, changing those in active voice to passive voice and vice versa.**

_____ **1.** Cats <u>inspire</u> writers. _____

_____ **2.** My cat B.K. <u>inspired</u> the songwriter who composed "I Did It My Way."

_____

_____ **3.** Mark Twain's favorite cats <u>were named</u> Beelzebub, Blatherskit, Apollinaris, and Buffalo Bill.

_____

_____

_____ **4.** The Cheshire Cat <u>gave</u> Alice orders when she was in Wonderland.

_____

_____ **5.** A cat <u>helped</u> Dick Whittington become mayor of London.

_____

_____ **6.** The poem "A Naming of Cats" <u>was written</u> by T. S. Eliot.

_____

_____ **7.** According to Rudyard Kipling, the cat <u>was</u> first <u>domesticated</u> by a cave woman.

_____

_____ **8.** Books about cats <u>are enjoyed</u> by most children.

_____

_____ **9.** Dr. Seuss <u>wrote</u> *The Cat in the Hat*, a book which has delighted young children since 1957.

_____

_____

Avoiding Misplaced Modifiers

Modifiers can be words, phrases, or clauses. In sentences, modifiers should be placed so that their meaning is clear. A **misplaced modifier** distorts or muddles sentence meaning.
Examples:

The lottery winner *almost* spent $50,000 on a new car.
The lottery winner spent *almost* $50,000 on a new car.

DIRECTIONS ▷ **Underline the misplaced modifier in each sentence. Rewrite the sentence to correct the modifier's placement.**

1. Butterflies with their forefeet taste things.

_____

2. Just like fingerprints do, footprints work.

_____

3. Bound feet in ancient China were a mark of highest beauty.

_____

4. Women who bound their feet could barely walk there.

_____

5. The tarantula on its feet has "noses."

_____

6. Only ostriches have two toes.

_____

7. As shovels moles use their feet.

_____

8. The lynx grows hairs for walking on snow on the bottoms of its feet.

_____

9. Mudskippers, faster than most people can walk, can hop.

_____

10. By suction the feet of starfish work.

_____

11. As feet they use hundreds of hollow tubes.

_____

Misplaced Modifiers

Consistent Verb Tenses

Careful writers avoid shifts in verb tense unless there is good reason.

DIRECTIONS ▷ **Rewrite the paragraphs, correcting any sentences containing a verb that is inconsistent with the rest of the paragraph. If there is a good reason for a shift in verb tense, explain it in writing.**

1. It was a bitter cold night for speed skating, but the three teams give their all for the regional competition. Most surprising was the performance of Coolidge High, which outskated the other two teams in every category. They are the easy winners.

_____

_____

_____

2. Johnson raced down the court. He stops dead, raises those incredibly long arms, and sinks the ball slow-motion into the basket. He scored 33 points before the final quarter ended.

_____

_____

_____

3. Golf has always been my dad's favorite game. He says it is easygoing, just like he is. He used to spend every Saturday and Sunday on the links when he was my age. He worked as a caddy to earn enough money to play golf himself.

_____

_____

_____

4. I had never seen a rodeo before. I expect the events to be tough and exciting. What I don't expect was the gracefulness and incredible agility involved. I was glued to my seat.

_____

_____

_____

_____

Troublesome Verbs

Certain verb pairs are frequently confused for one another.
Sit means "to take a seat, as in a chair." *Set* means "to put in a certain place or position."
Rise means "get up" or "move higher." *Raise* means "lift" or "elevate."
Lie means "to be or remain" or "to recline." *Lay* means "to put or place in a particular position."

Present Tense	Past Tense	Past Participle
lie	lay	(has, have, had) lain
lay	laid	(has, have, had) laid
sit	sat	(has, have, had) sat
set	set	(has, have, had) set
rise	rose	(has, have, had) risen
raise	raised	(has, have, had) raised

DIRECTIONS ▷ **Write the verb that completes each sentence correctly.**

1. (set, sat) Admiral Zorg _____ at the controls of the starship *Explorer*.

2. (set, sat) He had _____ the velocity of the ship at warp speed 7.

3. (lay, laid) Planet 32 of the Trifton solar system _____ in ruins.

4. (sat, set) The ship's navigator, Lieutenant Maxar, _____ at the admiral's side.

5. (rose, raised) Zorg _____ his arm wearily.

6. (lay, lain) Pointing to the remains of Planet 32, he said, "The volcano had _____ dormant for millennia."

7. (rise, raise) He added, "Who could have predicted that the lava would _____ so suddenly?"

8. (laid, lay) Maxar _____ a complex chart of numbers and symbols on the desk.

9. (lies, lays) "The answer _____ here in these probability calculations, Admiral," he said.

10. (Set, Sit) The admiral nodded sadly. "_____ our course for home," he ordered.

DIRECTIONS ▷ **Write a sentence using each of the following verbs correctly.**

11. sitting _____

12. setting _____

13. lying _____

14. laying _____

Writing for an Audience and Purpose

Careful writers are guided by their **purpose** for writing and their intended **audience**.

DIRECTIONS Each item below names an audience. Circle the letter of the passage that is better adapted for that audience.

1. six-year-olds
   a. The grieving process for the death of a family pet can be almost as stressful as it is for the death of a close relative.
   b. Dogs and cats do not live as long as people do. Sometimes pets die, and that makes us feel terrible.

2. scientists
   a. My cat Binky does the strangest thing! He makes a funny chattering sound whenever he sees a bird.
   b. Wild cats are quiet and stealthy when stalking birds. Pet cats, however, make a chattering sound in their throats.

3. potential buyers of pets
   a. This lovable little bundle of fur will be just like another member of your family.
   b. Canines do require more care than felines. For example, they must be exercised frequently.

DIRECTIONS Write one paragraph about the responsibilities of caring for a dog or cat for the audience listed.

4. adults: _____

_____

_____

_____

_____

5. fourth graders: _____

_____

_____

_____

_____

Personal Narrative

In a **personal narrative**, the writer tells about an event that the writer participated in or observed. A personal narrative is autobiographical, but it typically focuses on a specific experience. A personal narrative
- is written in the first-person point of view.
- usually reveals or suggests the writer's feelings.
- has a beginning, a middle, and an end.

DIRECTIONS ▷ **Read the personal narrative below. Then, answer the questions that follow.**

My early art was so bad that my first-grade teacher suggested my vision be tested. When the ophthalmologist gave me a clean bill of health, my parents sent me to an optometrist for eye-hand coordination exercises. Still, none of my artwork was ever posted on the classroom bulletin board.

At home, however, things were different. My parents proudly displayed on the refrigerator nearly every piece of art I ever produced. One time my father had an abstract that especially pleased him framed. Encouraged by my family, I continued to draw. My parents tell me I never seemed to notice that my drawings were very different from those of my classmates.

For my birthday, Granny bought me two books: *How to Draw Animals* and *How to Draw Space Creatures*. I began to practice, used some of the authors' ideas and some of my own, and developed a distinctive style. I started creating the things I'd always seen in my imagination.

1. From what point of view is this narrative told? _____

2. How do you know? _____

   _____

3. List the events of the narrative in the order in which they happened.

   a. _____

   b. _____

   c. _____

   d. _____

   e. _____

   f. _____

4. What do you think eventually happens in the writer's life? _____

   _____

5. What is the main theme the writer is trying to convey? _____

   _____

   _____

Writing from a Point of View

Careful writers choose a specific **point of view** and write only from that point of view unless there is a good reason to change.

◎◎◎◎ ◎◎◎◎◎◎◎◎◎◎◎◎◎◎◎◎◎◎◎◎◎◎◎◎◎◎◎◎◎◎◎◎◎◎◎◎◎◎

DIRECTIONS ▷ **After reading the passage, describe the scene from the points of view specified in the questions. Include feelings and reactions as well as observations in your narratives.**

There is a small, old house in the middle of a large garden. A stone wall surrounds the garden, which can be entered only through a tall iron gate. The house is a little run-down, but bright flowers grow everywhere.

1. Point of view: a young woman at the gate looking for a house to buy

_____

_____

_____

_____

_____

_____

2. Point of view: a child playing hide-and-seek in the garden

_____

_____

_____

_____

_____

_____

3. Point of view: a fox searching for its dinner

_____

_____

_____

_____

_____

_____

Personal Narrative: Graphic Organizer

 **DIRECTIONS** Plan to write a personal narrative about something you do well. Use the graphic organizer to plan your personal narrative.

What are you going to write about?

Tell what your skill is, how you learned it, and when you use it.

Tell how your skill makes your life more interesting.

Personal Narrative: Writing

Tips for Writing a Personal Narrative
- Write from your point of view. Use the words *I, me, my,* and *mine* to show your readers that this is your story.
- Think about what you want to tell your readers.
- Organize your ideas into a beginning, middle, and end.
- Write an interesting introduction that "grabs" your readers.
- Write an ending that expresses your point of view.

DIRECTIONS Write a personal narrative about something you do well. Use the graphic organizer on page 82 as a guide for writing. Be sure to proofread your writing.

_____

_____

_____

_____

_____

_____

_____

_____

_____

_____

_____

_____

_____

_____

_____

_____

_____

_____

_____

Evaluating a Personal Narrative

DIRECTIONS Use the chart below to evaluate a personal narrative. Check *Yes* or *No* to answer each question. If the answer is *No*, make notes about ways to revise and improve the narrative.

Question	Yes ✔	No ✔	If *No*, what needs to be done to improve the narrative?
Does the narrative describe something the writer does well?			
Does the narrative contain a beginning paragraph that captures the reader's attention?			
Does the writer describe how the skill was learned?			
Does the writer explain when the skill is used?			
Does the writer develop the content by adding interesting details?			
Does the writer make the subject interesting by using interesting vocabulary?			
Does the narrative contain an ending paragraph that closes the subject effectively?			
Is the narrative written in first person?			
Does the narrative reveal or suggest the writer's feelings?			
Has the writer corrected mistakes in spelling, grammar, and punctuation?			

DIRECTIONS Use the notes in the chart and the graphic organizer on page 82 to revise the narrative as needed. Use the information in Units 1–4 to correct grammar, usage, and mechanics problems.

Personal Narrative

Personal Narrative: Proofreading

To be a good proofreader, look for one type of error at a time. For example, proofread once for capitalization errors, once for punctuation errors, and once for spelling errors.

PROOFREADER'S MARKS

≡	Capitalize.	⌃	Replace something.
⊙	Add a period.	⸮	Transpose.
∧	Add something.	◯	Spell correctly.
⋏	Add a comma.	¶	Indent paragraph.
⌄⌄	Add quotation marks.	/	Make a lowercase letter.
⸝	Cut something.		

DIRECTIONS ▷ **Proofread this excerpt from a personal narrative. Use the proofreader's marks above to correct at least ten errors. Pay special attention to paragraph indentations.**

The first time your parents leave you at home alone is exciting for every child. I guess. In my case, however, there was a little more excitement than I had anticipated. I was 14, my sister Josie was 10, jeannie was seven, kathryn was six, and my brother Messy was just two. Mom and Dad were just going a few miles away to their favorite restaurant. It was their anniversary.

"I'll just tuck Messy into his crib," Mom said. "He'll probably go right to sleep." "Just try to keep things quiet here," added Dad. "We'll be back in about three hours." I was "in charge," and I felt pretty grown-up about it. The Romeros our next-door neighbors had been briefed by my parents and were watching us carefully.

That turned out to be a very good thing. My sisters and I were playing checkers when we heard a strange sound. It was a muffled roaring, and it seemed to get louder and louder. Luckily, the Romeros were soon banging on the door, and I was free to panic. "tornado!" boomed Mr. Romero. We raced to our rooms, threw blankets over our pajamas, grabbed Messy, and dashed to the Romeros' basement.

Compare and Contrast Paper

A **compare and contrast paper**
- describes the similarities and differences in two or more items or describes their advantages and disadvantages.
- addresses the same questions about each item.

⊙⊙⊙⊙⊙⊙⊙⊙⊙⊙⊙⊙⊙⊙⊙⊙⊙⊙⊙⊙⊙⊙⊙⊙⊙⊙⊙⊙⊙⊙⊙⊙⊙⊙⊙⊙

DIRECTIONS > **Analyze this excerpt from a compare and contrast paper. Then, answer the questions.**

Jogging is an aerobic exercise that gives your heart and your lungs a good workout. It uses very little special equipment, so it can be practiced at very little expense. Many people like jogging because it gets them out into the fresh air and provides new things to look at, so it's not as boring as some other forms of exercise. On the other hand, some doctors say that joggers can damage their joints with the pounding that jogging gives them. In addition, jogging can be dangerous if traffic is heavy. Besides the possibility of accidents, inhaling car fumes can present problems.

Rowing machines are also good sources of exercise. They provide an aerobic workout that exercises both legs and arms equally, and they also provide a good workout for the heart and lungs. Because people can use their machines indoors, they are not prevented from exercising in bad weather. On the other hand, people with bad knees may have trouble with all the bending involved. Rowing machines are expensive, and some people are bored by the repetitiveness of this form of exercise.

1. What is being compared? _____

   _____

2. Identify four points the writer addresses about each form of exercise.

   _____

   _____

   _____

   _____

3. Summarize the paragraphs by completing the chart below.

How jogging and rowing are alike	How jogging and rowing are different

⊙⊙⊙⊙⊙⊙⊙⊙⊙⊙⊙⊙⊙⊙⊙⊙⊙⊙⊙⊙⊙⊙⊙⊙⊙⊙⊙⊙⊙⊙⊙⊙⊙

Keeping to the Topic

Good writers focus their writing carefully. Coherence automatically results when all the content supports the main idea.

◎◎◎◎ ◎◎ ◎◎◎◎◎◎◎◎◎◎◎ ◎◎◎ ◎◎◎◎◎ ◎◎◎ ◎◎◎ ◎◎◎◎◎ ◎◎◎◎ ◎◎ ◎

DIRECTIONS ▷ **Read each paragraph. Underline the words or sentences that do not contribute to the main idea. Then, rewrite the paragraph so that it is a unified composition.**

1. All the students we interviewed said they were responsible for doing chores at home. Most boys were responsible for washing dishes and vacuuming. My brother and I used to switch tasks all the time. Both boys and girls were responsible for keeping their rooms clean. For both groups, this was the least favorite task. Years ago, boys had fewer household duties.

   _____

   _____

   _____

   _____

   _____

   _____

   _____

2. My room is sometimes messy, but my sister's room is always a total disaster area. One wall of her room is covered with her hat collection. Why would anyone want to collect hats? My walls are bare. I have a CD collection, but it is neatly stored in neat plastic racks. CDs are easier to collect and store than hats. Both my sister and I are pack rats, but my things are better organized. I hope I never have to share a room with my sister.

   _____

   _____

   _____

   _____

   _____

   _____

Compare and Contrast Paper: Graphic Organizer

DIRECTIONS ▷ Think about the music you like to listen to. How is it like the music your parents enjoy? How is it different? Plan to write a compare and contrast paper about how the two preferences are alike and different. Use the Venn diagram to help you plan your paper. List what is true only about A in the A circle. List what is true only about B in the B circle. List what is true about both A and B where the two circles overlap.

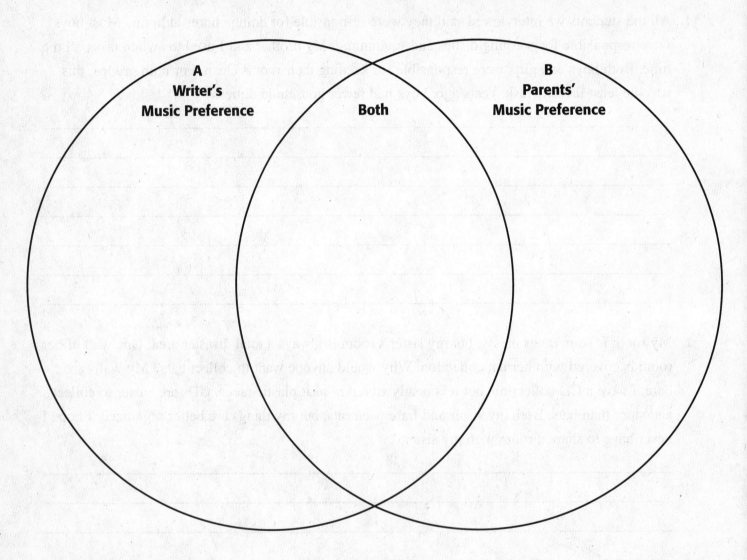

A
Writer's
Music Preference

Both

B
Parents'
Music Preference

Compare and Contrast Paper: Writing

Tips for Writing a Compare and Contrast Paper
- Find information about your subjects.
- Organize the information you find into main ideas.
- Use details to explain each main idea.
- Explain how the subjects are alike or what advantages they have.
- Explain how the subjects are different or what disadvantages they have.

DIRECTIONS Compare and contrast the music you like and the music your parents like. Use the Venn Diagram on page 88 as a guide for writing. Be sure to proofread your writing.

_____

_____

_____

_____

_____

_____

_____

_____

_____

_____

_____

_____

_____

_____

_____

_____

_____

_____

Evaluating a Compare and Contrast Paper

DIRECTIONS Use the chart below to evaluate a compare and contrast paper. Check *Yes* or *No* to answer each question. If the answer is *No*, make notes about ways to revise and improve the paper.

Question	Yes ✓	No ✓	If *No*, what needs to be done to improve the paper?
Does the writer introduce the subjects for comparison/contrast in the first paragraph?			
Does the writer explain how the two subjects are alike?			
Does the writer explain how the two subjects are different?			
Does the writer present more than one idea for each subject?			
Does the writer organize the ideas into paragraphs?			
Does the writer use details to support each point?			
Does the writer summarize the ideas in the paper's conclusion?			
Has the writer corrected mistakes in spelling, grammar, and punctuation?			

DIRECTIONS Use the notes in the chart and the graphic organizer on page 88 to revise the paper as needed. Use the information in Units 1–4 to correct grammar, usage, and mechanics problems.

Compare and Contrast Paper: Proofreading

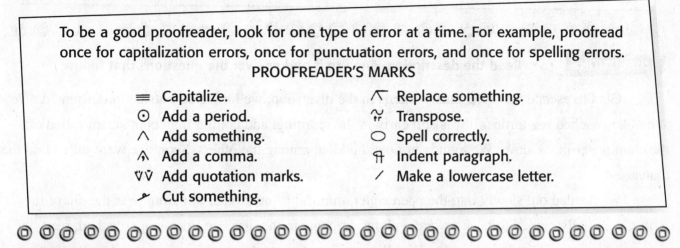

To be a good proofreader, look for one type of error at a time. For example, proofread once for capitalization errors, once for punctuation errors, and once for spelling errors.

PROOFREADER'S MARKS

≡ Capitalize.
⊙ Add a period.
∧ Add something.
⋏ Add a comma.
ᵛᵛ Add quotation marks.
✄ Cut something.

⋏ Replace something.
℣ Transpose.
○ Spell correctly.
⫟ Indent paragraph.
/ Make a lowercase letter.

DIRECTIONS ▷ **Proofread this excerpt from a compare and contrast paper. Use the proofreader's marks above to correct at least twelve errors. Pay special attention to punctuation of sentences.**

As people's awareness of animal rights has growed, so has the controversy over zoos. Collectors for zoos take animals away from their families and out on their natural habitats. They transport the animals long distances, often under difficult traveling conditions. Zoos are confining and animals that are placed in them may be prevented from following they're natural instincts. To supply the demand for wild creatures poachers catch some animals illegally. Certain exotic animals are disappearing from the wild altogether, upsetting the balance of Nature.

On the other hand zoos increase people's awareness of the uniqueness and diversity of the animal population. Many people did'nt begin to care about dolphins, and dolphin safety until they had seen these beautiful, playful animals at zoos or theme parks. Many people now appreciate the importance of the rain forests because they have encountered it's beautiful creatures. It if possible that zoo animals would be more happier in the wild. However, some natural habitats have disappeared so completly that, without the zoo population, many species would now be extinct. Perhaps we need zoos as a refuge.

Descriptive Story

A **descriptive story** contains comparisons, descriptive language, and sensory details.

DIRECTIONS Read the description. Analyze it and answer the questions that follow.

Glad to escape the stale, musty smells in the dive shop, we lumbered outside in our rented dive suits like beached sea turtles. It was still early in the morning, and coiling fingers of steam rolled off the calm water in the cove. We found our boat, huddled among the others. Soon, we were off to find the manatees!

We headed out slowly into the open water, mindful of our wake. Shouting over the din of the motor, we finally agreed to head toward a clump of boats in the distance. As we approached, we scanned the water for telltale bubbles. We all spotted it at once. A manatee was just below the surface ahead on the right! Without a moment's hesitation, two of us jumped over the gunwale into the warm water of Crystal River. We saw before us a large, brown "seacow," an apt name for this gentle creature. I had been assured I could touch it, but it was easily four times my size. Gingerly, I reached out and just brushed the manatee's leathery-skinned shoulder with my fingertips. The animal went right on ripping out giant mouthfuls of elodea, or sea grass, just like a living steam shovel. I had touched my first wild sea creature!

1. List a detail from the description that appeals to the following senses:

   sight _____

   smell _____

   hearing _____

   touch _____

2. Name two things in the description that are compared to something else. To what are they

   compared? _____

   _____

   _____

3. Underline six phrases in the description that show location.

Using Vivid Language

Skilled writers use vivid language in their descriptions.

DIRECTIONS > **Write three vivid words or phrases a writer might use in place of each common descriptive word. Use a thesaurus if you need help.**

1. quiet _____

2. big _____

3. soft _____

4. sour _____

5. red _____

6. cold _____

7. smelly _____

8. nervous _____

9. pale _____

10. thin _____

11. good _____

12. bad _____

13. happy _____

14. sad _____

15. beautiful _____

16. ugly _____

17. fast _____

18. slow _____

DIRECTIONS > **Rewrite these descriptions of people, using more vivid language.**

19. You always know when Rosa enters a room.

_____

20. Jim has an easy way with people.

_____

21. My little brother has a natural curiosity.

_____

Descriptive Story: Graphic Organizer

Plan to write a descriptive story about a trip to any planet in the universe or place in the world. Use the graphic organizer to plan the story. Write your subject in the center of the circle. Then, write words that describe the subject or experience on the lines.

Descriptive Story: Writing

Tips for Writing a Descriptive Story
- Use your voice when you write. That means you should use your special way of expressing yourself.
- Help readers see, smell, taste, feel, and hear what you are writing about.
- Use interesting words to help you describe.
- Use similes and metaphors to help your readers imagine the experience you are writing about.

DIRECTIONS Imagine that you could visit any planet in the universe or place in the world. Where would you go and what would you do? Write a descriptive story about your adventure. Use the graphic organzier on page 94 as a guide for writing. Be sure to proofread your writing.

_____
_____
_____
_____
_____
_____
_____
_____
_____
_____
_____
_____
_____
_____
_____
_____

Evaluating a Descriptive Story

DIRECTIONS ▷ Use the chart below to evaluate a descriptive story. Check *Yes* or *No* to answer each question. If the answer is *No*, make notes about ways to revise and improve the story.

Question	Yes ✔	No ✔	If *No*, what needs to be done to improve the story?
Does the writer describe the sights, sounds, smells, tastes, and feel of the experience?			
Does the writer use a unique way of expressing himself or herself?			
Does the writer include vocabulary that is vivid and interesting?			
Does the writer use similes and metaphors to help readers imagine the experience?			
Does the writer use action words to describe what happens?			
Has the writer corrected mistakes in spelling, grammar, and punctuation?			

DIRECTIONS ▷ Use the notes in the chart and the graphic organzier on page 94 to revise the descriptive story as needed. Use the information in Units 1–4 to correct grammar, usage, and mechanics problems.

Descriptive Story: Proofreading

To be a good proofreader, look for one type of error at a time. For example, proofread once for capitalization errors, once for punctuation errors, and once for spelling errors.

PROOFREADER'S MARKS

≡ Capitalize.
⊙ Add a period.
∧ Add something.
⋏ Add a comma.
∨∨ Add quotation marks.
⤷ Cut something.

⌃ Replace something.
⩕ Transpose.
○ Spell correctly.
⊬ Indent paragraph.
/ Make a lowercase letter.

DIRECTIONS ▷ **Proofread the description. Use the proofreader's marks above to correct at least fifteen errors.**

I woke in the early morning. The planit's three suns, shining through the sides of the tent, created a strange, orange glow in the air. It was bitterly cold. I lay in my down, sleeping bag, watching my breath frost in front of my eyes. there was not a sound, not a stirring of wind not a bird, not a crack of a twig. It was the kind of quite that made me think of danger, and that was a thought I did not need on this still freezing morning millions miles from home.

I unfurled the stiff, gray cover to the little window in the side of the tent, which I could just reach from the sleeping bag. Outside was a landscape of snow and ice, blue and purple below the sky's dim, orange glow. Heavy straight growths, almost like tree trunks, stuck up out of the snow. None of them had any branches or twigs or, presumably, leafs. We had not even determined weather they were living things. They were the only features in a landscape of ice and rock.

A low, jagged mountain shimmered in the distance. Crystal mound was it's name. I knew it was formed of strange crystalline shapes of rose, turquoise, and yellow, though its colors looked washed out at this distance. I also knowed that it was growing. We scientists had watched it grow. It was, strangely enough, the only thing on this silent planet that did seem to expand or change. As I watched, the beams from the Sun Major struck the mound, and a shimmering sparkling light shot out of it, dancing on the plain on snow.

How-To Paper

A **how-to paper**
- explains a process or procedure.
- introduces the subject in a topic sentence.
- lists the required materials *before* describing the steps.
- precisely states the steps to be taken, in order.

The skillful use of **precise vocabulary** and **time-order words** and phrases is essential in a how-to paper.

| DIRECTIONS | **Something is missing in each how-to example below. Analyze the examples and identify the missing element. Write it on the line.** |

1. Changing a flat tire is not difficult. Before you begin, read the instructions about how to use your jack. Loosen the lug nuts while the flat is still on the ground. Then position the jack correctly and jack up the car. Next, unscrew the lugs the rest of the way and remove the flat tire. Replace it with your spare tire. Then screw the lugs as tightly as possible. Finally, release the jack, and you're ready to go!

   _____

2. All you need is an address and a ZIP code directory. First, at a post office ask to see the directory of ZIP codes. Next, look in the directory for the state your letter is going to. Now, within the state listing, find the one you want. Finally, if it is a large city, you will also have to find the street. The ZIP codes are listed in the right column. Just copy the one you want onto your letter, and it's ready for the mailbox.

   _____

3. Giving a cat a pill can be difficult. Have these things ready: the pill, a towel, and a friend! Pick up your cat and pet it. Wrap the towel around the cat. Let your friend hold the cat firmly. Put your index fingers and thumbs on a corner of the cat's mouth. Pinch gently until the mouth opens. Place the pill on the back of the cat's mouth. Pinch gently until the mouth opens. Place the pill on the back of the cat's tongue. Close the cat's mouth and hold it shut until the cat swallows.

   _____

4. You can make money for your club or organization by having a community bake sale. Compile a list of volunteers to make baked goods, to contact merchants, and to sell the items. Be sure to have a table for displaying the goods, chairs for the cashiers, a metal box for money, and plenty of change. Find a good location.

Connecting Ideas in Sequence

To write a how-to paragraph, careful writers
- make a "movie" in their minds of the steps involved in the process.
- write the steps in the order in which they "see" them.
- use time-order words to make the sequence clear.
- ensure that the sequence is complete from beginning to end.

DIRECTIONS The steps below for washing a car are listed out of order. In the diagram, write the steps in the correct order. Add two steps that are missing.

Use window cleaner to clean the windows.

Rinse all soapsuds completely using a garden hose.

Vacuum the inside of the car.

Mix detergent with warm water in a bucket.

Gather all the equipment you will need.

Begin all work at the top of the car and work downward.

Step 1	Step 5
Step 2	Step 6
Step 3	Step 7
Step 4	Step 8

Using Precise Vocabulary

Skillful writers use precise language to make instructions clear.

DIRECTIONS **Read this how-to paragraph. Rewrite it, replacing vague words with precise words. Make up any amounts and measurements you may need.**

Would you like to grow vegetables even though you don't have space in your yard? You can still do it, using containers. Here's how to grow sugar-baby watermelons. Put some dirt into a large tub. Mix in some fertilizer. Also, rig up something for the vines to grow on. Plant the seeds and water them. Place the tub somewhere outside. When the melons are getting heavy, tie them up to the stakes with material so that the weight of the melons won't snap the vines. Sit back and watch your melons grow.

_____

_____

_____

_____

_____

_____

_____

_____

_____

_____

_____

_____

_____

_____

_____

_____

_____

_____

_____

How-To Paper: Graphic Organizer

 **DIRECTIONS** Think of a task you do often. It may be a job you enjoy or one you dislike. Use the graphic organizer to plan a how-to paper. Adjust the number of steps as needed.

Topic Sentence: _____

Step 1

Step 5

Step 2

Step 6

Step 3

Step 7

Step 4

Step 8

How-To Paper: Writing

Tips for Writing a How-To Paper
- Narrow the focus of the process or procedure you choose.
- Be sure the list of materials is complete.
- Be sure you have included every step in the process and that they are in correct sequence.
- Use time-order words as needed.
- Use precise vocabulary throughout the paper.

DIRECTIONS Write a how-to paper describing a task you do often. It may be a job you enjoy or one you dislike. Use the graphic organizer on page 101 as a guide. Proofread your paper carefully.

_____

_____

_____

_____

_____

_____

_____

_____

_____

_____

_____

_____

_____

_____

_____

_____

_____

_____

Evaluating a How-To Paper

DIRECTIONS Use the chart below to evaluate a how-to paper. Check *Yes* or *No* to answer each question. If the answer is *No*, make notes about ways to revise and improve the paper.

Question	Yes ✔	No ✔	If *No*, what needs to be done to improve the paper?
Does the writer introduce the subject or problem in a topic sentence?			
Does the writer provide a complete and precise list of the materials required?			
Does the list of materials precede the steps of the process?			
Are the steps presented in order?			
Is the list of steps complete?			
Does the writer use time-order words appropriately?			
Does the writer use precise vocabulary throughout the paper?			
Does the writer seem to be experienced and knowledgeable in performing this task?			
After reading the paper, will readers understand the process or still have questions?			
Has the writer corrected mistakes in spelling, grammar, and punctuation?			

DIRECTIONS Use the notes in the chart and the graphic organzier on page 101 to revise the paper as needed. Use the information in Units 1–4 to correct grammar, usage, and mechanics problems.

How-To Paper: Proofreading

To be a good proofreader, look for one type of error at a time. For example, proofread once for capitalization errors, once for punctuation errors, and once for spelling errors.

PROOFREADER'S MARKS

≡	Capitalize.	⌃	Replace something.
⊙	Add a period.	⤮	Transpose.
∧	Add something.	◯	Spell correctly.
⋏	Add a comma.	⁋	Indent paragraph.
⌵⌵	Add quotation marks.	/	Make a lowercase letter.
✗	Cut something.		

DIRECTIONS **Proofread these two excerpts from how-to papers. Use the proofreader's marks above to correct at least eighteen errors. Pay special attention to misspelled words.**

As the holidays approach, do you dread all those ours you will spend rapping gifts Your worries may be over. Wrapping presents for your family and friends can be an enjoyable expereince of you follow these simple rules. First, by all your wrapping supplies early. Go to a well-stocked paper store and buy these items: gift wrap, ribbon, tape tissue paper, and gift tags. Keep all your wrapping supplies together in one big bag. then wrap as you go. Each time you buy a present, pull out your speical bag and wrap the gift. When the write time comes, enjoy giving your beautifully wrapped presents.

Wrapping a package that contains breakibles takes patients and the right wrapping materials. First, find a sturdy box a few inches larger than the object you are mailing. Then buy plastick bubble wrap or Styrofoam "peanuts." Surround the object on all sides with padding and be sure it cannot move within the box. Then use strong, touff tape to seal the box. Finally, be sure to write FRAJILE on the box in large cleer letters. so everyone who handles your package will know it contians something breakable.

Persuasive Essay

A **persuasive essay**
- states an opinion or position on an issue.
- provides facts and reasons to support the opinion.
- contains arguments that appeal to the reader's ethics, emotions, or reason.
- has an introductory paragraph, supporting paragraphs, and a conclusion.

DIRECTIONS ▶ **Read and analyze this persuasive essay. Then, answer the questions.**

Should We Kick Out Football?

I am a sports nut. I spend hours glued to the television watching games—hockey, basketball, baseball, and football. I also play on the school's basketball and baseball teams. However, this sports fan has had enough of high school football. At the risk of being shunned by my friends, I say we should kick out football.

If you are growling at me as you read this, let me say that two months ago I would have been on your side. Two months ago, however, I hadn't read my dad's newsletter from the Riverton City Sports Council. The newsletter printed statistics about sports-related injuries in our state's schools. Football causes four hundred times as many injuries as any other sport. Last year, two local players suffered spinal cord injuries. One of those football players is in a wheelchair. He'll never walk again.

Students who play football are taking a terrible chance. One-third of the players sustain some kind of injury during the season. Do you think the new helmets protect players from serious hurt? Wrong! I don't know whether the players are practicing without helmets, or the helmets themselves are inadequate. I do know that 22 student football players in our state suffered head injuries last year. By contrast, only one basketball player in the whole state sustained a head injury.

1. What opinion or position does the writer state in this essay? _____

_____

2. In what part of the essay does that opinion appear? _____

_____

3. What type of appeal does the writer use? _____

_____

_____

4. Does the essay convince you to agree with its point of view? Why or why not? _____

_____

_____

_____

Supporting an Opinion

In a persuasive essay, writers use **legitimate reasons** to persuade their readers.

ⓞ ⓞⓞⓞ ⓞⓞⓞ ⓞⓞⓞⓞ ⓞⓞⓞ ⓞⓞⓞ ⓞⓞⓞ ⓞⓞⓞ ⓞⓞⓞ ⓞⓞⓞ ⓞⓞⓞ ⓞⓞⓞ ⓞⓞⓞ ⓞⓞⓞ

DIRECTIONS ▷ **Read the three reasons given to support each opinion. Write *legitimate reason* on the line beside the correct choice. For the other two choices, write a term from the box that identifies why each fails to support the stated opinion.**

faulty generalization	testimonial	bandwagon technique	**WORD BOX**
ignoring the question	labeling	faulty cause and effect	

1. An Airedale is the dog for you.

   a. All the movie stars are buying them. _____

   b. They are intelligent dogs and need little exercise room. _____

   c. The president says Airedales are his favorite dog. _____

2. Betty Silvers would make a good judge at a dog show.

   a. She raises dogs herself and has lots of experience through her work with the AKA. _____

   _____

   b. She is a cold fish and won't let feelings of friendship influence her decision. _____

   _____

   c. Right after she joined the advertising committee, they came up with a great ad campaign.

   _____

3. Everyone who has a dog should take it through obedience school.

   a. Mr. Klein's beagle loved going to obedience school. It was fun for dogs. _____

   b. Statistics on dog bites show that only 2 percent of dogs that bite have been through obedience

   school. _____

   c. My teacher took her dog through obedience training, and if it's good enough for her, it's good

   enough for me. _____

4. An animal shelter is a good place to find a new dog.

   a. Pit bulls do not make good pets. _____

   b. The animal shelter in our town picks up over 500 abandoned dogs each year. _____

   c. In an animal shelter, you can usually find a dog that has already been trained. _____

   _____

ⓞⓞ ⓞⓞⓞ ⓞⓞ ⓞⓞⓞ ⓞⓞⓞ ⓞⓞⓞ ⓞⓞⓞ ⓞⓞⓞ ⓞⓞⓞ ⓞⓞⓞ ⓞⓞⓞ ⓞⓞⓞ ⓞⓞ

Persuasive Essay: Graphic Organizer

DIRECTIONS Many people think that everyone should learn at least one language other than English. Should students be required to learn a foreign language to graduate from high school? Plan to write a persuasive essay expressing your opinion. Use the graphic organizer to help you plan.

What is the topic of your essay?

_____

_____

_____

What is your opinion on this topic?

_____

_____

_____

Reason 1

_____

_____

_____

_____

Why? Support your reason.

_____

_____

_____

_____

Reason 2

_____

_____

_____

_____

Why? Support your reason.

_____

_____

_____

_____

Reason 3

_____

_____

_____

_____

Why? Support your reason.

_____

_____

_____

_____

Persuasive Essay: Writing

Tips for Writing a Persuasive Essay
• Grab your reader's attention in the first paragraph.
• State your opinion clearly.
• Support your opinion with legitimate arguments and clear examples.
• Present your examples from least important to most important.
• Use the last paragraph to summarize your essay.
• Use your last paragraph to leave the reader convinced you are right.

DIRECTIONS Should students be required to learn a foreign language to graduate from high school? Write a persuasive essay expressing your opinion. Use the graphic organizer on page 107 as a guide for writing. Be sure to proofread your writing.

_____

_____

_____

_____

_____

_____

_____

_____

_____

_____

_____

_____

_____

_____

_____

_____

_____

_____

Evaluating a Persuasive Essay

 Use the chart below to evaluate a persuasive essay. Check *Yes* or *No* to answer each question. If the answer is *No*, make notes about ways to revise and improve the essay.

Question	Yes ✔	No ✔	If *No*, what needs to be done to improve the essay?
Does the writer state his or her opinion clearly?			
Does the writer grab the reader's attention in the first paragraph?			
Does the writer provide legitimate arguments for the opinion?			
Does the essay include facts, statistics, or examples to support the arguments?			
Does the writer avoid faulty generalizations, testimonials, labeling, use of the bandwagon technique, and faulty cause and effect?			
Does the writer present arguments from least to most important?			
Does the writer appeal to the reader's ethics, emotions, or reason?			
Does the writer summarize his or her position in the last paragraph?			
Does the essay convince the reader of the writer's position?			
Has the writer corrected mistakes in spelling, grammar, and punctuation?			

 Use the notes in the chart and the graphic organzier on page 107 to revise the essay as needed. Use the information in Units 1–4 to correct grammar, usage, and mechanics problems.

Persuasive Essay: Proofreading

To be a good proofreader, look for one type of error at a time. For example, proofread once for capitalization errors, once for punctuation errors, and once for spelling errors.

PROOFREADER'S MARKS

≡ Capitalize.
⊙ Add a period.
∧ Add something.
⩘ Add a comma.
ᵛⱽ Add quotation marks.
⟋ Cut something.

⌃ Replace something.
ᔍ Transpose.
◯ Spell correctly.
Ħ Indent paragraph.
⁄ Make a lowercase letter.

DIRECTIONS ▷ **Proofread this excerpt from a persuasive essay. Use the proofreader's marks above to correct at least fifteen errors. Pay special attention to capitalization of proper nouns.**

The people of the World are faced with alarming environmental problems. I am convinced that we must all cooperate through international agencys to solve these problems. Working alone, one state or or one nation cannot protect it's land and people from environmental hazards. The problems faced by people in the united states are also problems for people in canada, Japan, and russia. Only by facing these problems together and trying to work out cooperative solutions can we protect ourself and our Planet.

International cooperation is needed for several reasons. in the first place, some environmental dangers threaten the whole planet rather than local areas. Damage to the ozone layer is a good example. If someone in nebraska uses an aerosol spray, the chemicals do not stay in Nebraska. Those damaging chemicals travel to the ozone layer, where they effect the hole world. Therefore, a State or Country cannot protect itself against ozone damage simply by passing a law forbidding the local use of aerosols.

Capturing the Reader's Interest

Skilled writers capture the reader's interest by
- creating a good title.
- using a catchy beginning.
- creating a satisfying ending.

DIRECTIONS Circle the letter of the best title for a personal narrative. Write a sentence explaining why you think that title is best.

1. **a.** My First Day of School
   b. How I Broke My Leg (and Put My Foot in My Mouth)
   c. August 27, 2003

   _____

2. **a.** Terror!
   b. My Most Frightening Experience
   c. How I Escaped from the Leopard

   _____

3. **a.** The School Play
   b. Starring Harry Lee as an Oak Tree!
   c. My First Part in a Play

   _____

DIRECTIONS Put a check mark next to the story beginning with the better "hook." Write a sentence explaining why you chose it.

4. _____ This was going to be the end of life as I knew it. What a mistake!

   _____ I made a big mistake when I was 12 years old.

   _____

   _____

5. _____ Did you ever wake up just knowing something special was about to happen?

   _____ When I woke up, I knew it would be a special day.

   _____

   _____

Varying Sentence Length

Careful writers vary the length of their sentences by
- avoiding too many short, choppy sentences.
- avoiding too many long, complicated sentences.
- combining choppy sentences to make longer, smoother sentences.
- shortening or dividing long, complicated sentences.

⊙⊙⊙⊙ ⊙⊙⊙ ⊙⊙⊙⊙ ⊙⊙⊙ ⊙⊙⊙ ⊙⊙⊙ ⊙⊙⊙ ⊙⊙⊙ ⊙⊙⊙ ⊙⊙⊙ ⊙⊙⊙ ⊙⊙⊙ ⊙⊙⊙ ⊙⊙⊙ ⊙⊙⊙ ⊙⊙ ⊙⊙ ⊙

DIRECTIONS ▷ **Rewrite this paragraph. Combine short, choppy sentences to create a smooth writing style, and divide sentences that are too long or complex.**

Last week, I came to your store. I bought an exercise bike. The sales clerk informed me that delivery would be made within seven days. Seven days passed. No delivery was made. I called customer service. Because I had kept the receipt from the week before, I was able to give the customer service people the invoice number of the sale, and they, in turn, were able to trace the record of the sale, which was still in the sporting goods department. Then I talked with the manager of sporting goods. He told me that the store does not deliver to my town. I am angry.

_____

_____

_____

_____

_____

_____

_____

_____

_____

_____

_____

_____

_____

_____

⊙⊙⊙ ⊙⊙⊙ ⊙⊙⊙ ⊙⊙⊙ ⊙⊙⊙ ⊙⊙ ⊙⊙⊙ ⊙⊙⊙ ⊙⊙⊙ ⊙⊙⊙ ⊙⊙⊙ ⊙

Using Formal and Informal Language

Skillful writers change their writing to use
- an appropriately formal and serious tone in research reports and other formal compositions.
- an informal and casual tone in less serious writing.

DIRECTIONS Write *formal* or *informal* to identify the language in each sentence. Then, rewrite the sentence. If it is formal writing, make it informal. If it is informal, make it formal.

1. Carnivorous plants use an unorthodox method of obtaining nutrients.

_____

2. They trap insects inside specially constructed plant structures, which then secrete digestive juices.

_____

_____

_____

3. Since these plants are incapable of stalking their prey, they have developed snares.

_____

_____

4. Sundews have leaves like little spoons, with sticky hairs on the edges.

_____

_____

5. Teeny flying bugs that use the hairs as a landing field are stuck forever on their gooey surfaces.

_____

_____

6. Butterworts' leaves practically drip "butter," a gooey stuff for catching bugs.

_____

_____

7. Terrariums offer a perfect environment for most carnivorous plants.

_____

_____

Writing for a Test

Writing for a test requires special skills. Usually the writer has no choice of topic; the topic is assigned. Often there is a time limit during which all stages of the writing process must be carried out. Keeping in mind any such restrictions, you should build in the time to plan and revise your writing. Thinking about these questions may help:

PREWRITING

Choosing a Topic
- What questions must I answer?
- Am I being asked to compare, give an opinion, explain, analyze, or describe?
- What kind of writing will fulfill this assignment?

Gathering Information
- Am I allowed to refer to my textbook?
- Can I make a rough outline to help organize my thoughts?

DRAFTING

- What will I use as my topic sentence?
- How much time do I have to finish the draft? How many minutes should I allot to each question or essay?

RESPONDING AND REVISING

- Have I answered the question completely?
- Are there any additional facts I should include?

PROOFREADING

- Have I spelled every word correctly?
- Are my sentences grammatically correct?

PUBLISHING

- Do I have time to rewrite this neatly?

Writing Prompts

Many schools use tests to evaluate students' ability to write. One kind of test uses a **writing prompt**, which requires a written response to a statement, a question, or a picture. Careful reading of the prompt will help determine the writing form, the audience (if given), and the purpose for writing (to inform, to persuade, to entertain, to describe). Often students are supplied with enough paper to plan and write the response.

Example:

Prompt	**Some people say exercise not only keeps you fit but also can give you more energy and better concentration. Do you agree or disagree? Write an essay in which you state your opinion and support it with at least one example.**
Organizing notes	*Does exercise keep me fit, boost my energy, and help me concentrate? Yes.* *Example of this: my swimming* *Reasons why (or how?) it helps:* *1. the exercise gives me energy* *2. easier to concentrate when I've exercised*
Thesis statement	*Frequent exercise can help improve your energy level and concentration.*

DIRECTIONS ▷ **Choose one of the writing prompts below. Follow the tips on pages 114 and 116 to prepare your written response to the prompt.**

1. What are your two favorite TV shows? Think about the characters, plots, and settings. Write a paper that tells how the two shows are alike and how they are different.

2. The school board is considering buying uniforms for everyone at your school. They say wearing uniforms will help students concentrate on their studies. What is your opinion? Write a persuasive essay for the school newspaper to convince others that your opinion is the right one.

3. Think of the best thing that ever happened to you. When did it happen? Where were you? What made it so wonderful? Write a story about the best thing that ever happened to you. Be sure to include details that help your readers picture the events in the story.

4. Imagine that you are camping in a forest. The sun is shining through the trees, but a summer storm is on the way. Make notes about what you see, hear, feel, smell, and taste as you wait for the storm. Write a descriptive story using this setting.

Essay Questions

Many tests include **essay questions**. The test taker must divide the given time into time to plan, time to draft, and time to revise each answer.
Example:

How did Native Americans adapt to their environment? Give two examples.

Inuit—igloos, travel for food   2
Iroquois—homes of wood and bark, hunted game 1

Freewrite facts and ideas
Organize by numbering facts in logical order

Topic sentence: Native Americans had to adapt their housing and eating habits to their environment.

Develop main idea for topic

Native Americans had to adapt their housing and eating habits to their environment. The Iroquois lived in the Eastern forests, where trees and game animals were plentiful. They built houses called longhouses out of wood and bark. An example of adaptation to extreme conditions is the Inuit way of life. In the Arctic, many Inuit built igloos for winter homes. They, too, traveled in search of food.

Write

Tips for Writing for a Test:
• Freewrite facts and ideas.
• Organize by numbering facts in logical order.
• Develop main idea for topic.
• Write.

Kinds of Books

The library has different kinds of books. The book groups are usually housed in separate sections or rooms in the library.

Fiction books include novels and short stories.

Nonfiction books tell facts about real people, things, or events. A **biography** is a nonfiction book that tells about the life of a real person.

A **periodical** is a published work that appears in a series. Newspapers and magazines are periodicals.

Reference books, such as encyclopedias, dictionaries, and thesauruses, are good sources of information on many subjects.

DIRECTIONS Write *fiction, nonfiction, biography, periodical,* or *reference* to identify the type of book described in each question.

1. the novel *Maniac Magee* _____

2. the *Merriam Webster Dictionary* _____

3. a book about the history of the National Park Service _____

4. an encyclopedia article about Camp David _____

5. a magazine from the American Camping Association _____

6. maps of camping areas in your state _____

7. a book titled *Scary Stories from Around the Campfire* _____

8. a book titled *The Synonym Finder* _____

9. a book titled *How to Set Up a Campsite* _____

10. a book titled *Bartlett's Familiar Quotations* _____

11. a newspaper article about summer camps _____

12. a book that tells about the life of Juliette Low _____

13. the book *Harry Potter and the Sorcerer's Stone* _____

14. a book titled *Information Please Almanac* _____

15. a book titled *Lincoln: A Photobiography* _____

16. a book titled *Artcyclopedia* _____

The Parts of a Book

The **title page** tells the name of the book, its author, and the name of the company that published the book.

The **copyright page** is on the back of the title page. It tells when the book was published.

The **acknowledgments page** names those who helped develop the book's content. It officially recognizes the contributions made by sources other than the author.

The **foreword/preface** contains introductory comments about the book. It can be written by the author or someone else.

The **contents page** lists the titles of the chapters or units in the book and the pages on which they begin.

The **glossary** contains definitions of difficult or unfamiliar words that appear in the book.

The **bibliography** is a list of books about a certain subject. It can also be a list of books the author used or referred to in the text.

The **index** is a list of all the topics in a book. It is in alphabetical order and lists the page or pages on which each topic appears.

▶ DIRECTIONS **Identify the part of a book where the following information can be found.**

1. To find the meaning of a technical term used in a book, you would look in the _____.

2. If you want to do further reading about a subject, you would consult the book's _____.

3. You want to know if the book you are reading is up-to-date. To find out when the book was published, you would look on the _____.

4. A friend hands you a book called *Back to My Roots*, and you wonder if Alex Haley is the author. Where in the book would you look? _____

5. You want to know who helped Alex Haley research his story. To find out, you would read the _____.

6. You are researching the history of Gambia, but the *Encyclopedia of World History* doesn't have a chapter on that country. Where else in the book would you look to see if Gambia is mentioned in the book? _____

7. Where would you find the name of a book's publisher? _____

8. Charles Dickens' *A Tale of Two Cities* was published in 1859. In the most recent edition of this famous classic, an expert on Victorian literature has been asked to provide new information about Dickens' life. Where would you look for this content? _____

9. You are looking for books about life in traditional African villages in the 1700s. The librarian hands you a stack of books. Where would you look first to select books that suit your purposes? _____

Using a Table of Contents

A **table of contents** lists the titles of the chapters or units in a book and gives the pages on which they begin. Contents pages can help readers examine the subjects covered in a book.

 **DIRECTIONS** Read this table of contents for a science book about oceans. Answer the questions that follow.

1. In which chapter would you find information about whales, dolphins, and sea otters? _____
   How do you know? _____

2. In which chapter would you expect to find pictures of the damage caused by an oil slick? _____
   What makes you think so? _____

3. Which is the longest chapter? _____

4. In which chapter might you find out how coral reefs are formed? _____

5. You're interested in finding out what kinds of seaweed grow near the coastlines. Where would
   you look? _____

6. You want to find out what the word *salinity* means. Where might you find it in this book?

   _____

7. In which chapter might you find information about pelicans? _____

8. You want to learn which creatures live in the deepest parts of the ocean. Which chapter would you
   read? _____

9. Which is the shortest chapter? _____

10. In which chapter would you find out what valuable things we can get from the oceans? _____

Using an Index

Many nonfiction books and most encyclopedias have an **index** of subject titles, listed in alphabetical order. The index shows the volume and the page number where an article can be found. Some encyclopedias contain articles on many different topics. Other encyclopedias contain different articles relating to a broad topic.

DIRECTIONS Use the sample encyclopedia index to answer the questions below.

Index
Acorn Squash, **1**–6; **11**–1759
     Baked, supreme, **1**–7
     Steamed, **1**–7
Appetizer(s), **1**–841; *see also* Cocktail; Dip; Pickle and Relish; Spread
     Almonds, **1**–89
     Celery, stuffed, **1**–89
     Cheese Ball, **3**–429
Cabbage, **2**–256; *see also* Salads, Coleslaw; Sauerkraut
     with bacon and cheese sauce, **1**–68
Flour, **5**–705
     Peanut, **8**–1328
     Rice, **10**–1556
     Wheat, **12**–1935

1. In what volume would you find an article on stuffed celery? _____

2. On what page would you find information on cabbage with bacon and cheese sauce? _____

3. Are all articles on flour found in the same volume? _____

4. What are the cross-references for **Appetizers**? _____

_____

5. Do the words in bold show the name of the volume or the name of the main food or ingredient?

_____

6. Which main food or ingredient has articles in two volumes? _____

7. Information on which appetizers can be found in the same volume and on the same page? _____

_____

8. What main ingredient is found in Volume 5? _____

9. If you looked under **Dip**, what might you expect to find as a cross-reference? _____

_____

10. Information on what appetizer would be found in Volume 3? _____

Using a Dictionary

A **dictionary** lists words in alphabetical order, giving their pronunciation, part of speech, and definition. Each word in the dictionary is called an **entry word**. Two **guide words** are located at the top of every dictionary page. The word on the left is the first entry word on that page, and the word on the right is the last entry word.

DIRECTIONS ▷ **Read the dictionary entries and answer the questions that follow.**

nation	nature

na·tion [nā´shən] *n.* **1** A group of people who live in a particular area, have a distinctive way of life, and are organized under a central government. They usually speak the same language. **2** A tribe or federation: the Iroquois *nation*.

na·tion·al [nash´ən·əl] **1** *adj.* Of, belonging to, or having to do with a nation as a whole: A *national* law; a *national* crisis. **2** *n.* a citizen of a nation. **–na´tion·al·ly** *adv.*

na·tion·wide [nā´shən·wīd´] *adj.* Extending throughout or across a nation.

na·tive [nā´tiv] **1** *adj.* Born, grown, or living naturally in a particular area. **2** *n.* A person, plant, or animal native to an area. **3** *n.* One of the original inhabitants of a place; aborigine. **4** *adj.* Related or belonging to a person by birth or place of birth: one's *native* language.

Native American One of or a descendant of the peoples living in the Western Hemisphere before the first Europeans came.

na·tive-born [nā´tiv·bôrn´] *adj.* Born in the area or country stated: a *native-born* Floridian.

1. What part of speech is *nation*? _____

2. What part of speech is *native-born*? _____

3. What is the meaning of *nationwide*? _____

_____

4. What is the base word of *nationally*? _____

5. Which meaning of the word *nation* is used in the following sentence?

Wilma Mankiller is the first woman to become chief of the Cherokee *nation*.

_____

6. What is the entry word for *nationally*? _____

7. How many syllables does *nationwide* have? _____

8. Would *natural* be found on the page with the guide words shown above? _____

Using a Thesaurus

A **thesaurus** is a book that gives synonyms, words that have nearly the same meaning, and antonyms, words that mean the opposite of a word. Many thesauruses are like dictionaries. The entry words are listed in dark print in alphabetical order. Guide words at the top of the page tell which words can be found on the page. Use a thesaurus to enrich your vocabulary and make your writing more colorful.

◎ ◎◎ ◎◎ ◎◎◎ ◎◎ ◎◎ ◎◎◎ ◎◎◎ ◎◎◎ ◎ ◎◎ ◎◎◎ ◎◎ ◎◎ ◎◎ ◎◎ ◎

DIRECTIONS ▷ **Rewrite each sentence. Use a thesaurus to replace the underlined word.**

1. Henry's heart <u>beat</u> as the ship pushed forward.

_____

2. The waves <u>grew</u> higher while the ship turned toward the storm, as if to meet it head-on.

_____

3. Henry's first voyage as a working sailor was already more <u>exciting</u> than his wildest dreams.

_____

4. The black clouds <u>hung</u> overhead, but the captain seemed to ignore them.

_____

5. The wind <u>blew</u> against the sails and plunged the ship in and out of foaming white water.

_____

6. A cold chill reached Henry's skin from deep inside his stomach, as his excitement turned to <u>fear</u>.

_____

7. High up on the ship's bridge, the <u>experienced</u> captain looked down at the crew working on the

deck. _____

_____

8. <u>Seeing</u> the look of fear on young Henry's face, the captain suddenly descended to the deck.

_____

9. He wanted to <u>tell</u> the crew that the storm would soon pass and the sea would become calm once

again. _____

_____

10. But who can really soothe an inexperienced sailor who is about to <u>face</u> his first raging storm?

_____

◎ ◎◎ ◎◎ ◎◎◎◎◎◎ ◎ ◎ ◎◎◎◎ ◎◎◎ ◎◎ ◎◎ ◎◎ ◎◎◎◎ ◎

Using an Encyclopedia

An **encyclopedia** is a set of reference books, each of which is called a **volume**. Each volume contains many articles on various topics. The topics are arranged alphabetically, and the spine of each volume indicates which articles are within. For example, a spine that is labeled *N-O* indicates that the volume has articles beginning with the letters *N* and *O*. At the end of most articles, related topics are listed. These listed items are called **cross-references**. Often you can find more information about your topic in these articles.

DIRECTIONS Read the entry for *armadillo* in an encyclopedia and answer the following questions.

1. Where do armadillos live? _____

2. What do they eat? _____

3. How do they protect themselves? _____

4. How much do they weigh? _____

DIRECTIONS Read the entry for *Sir Edmund Hillary* in an encyclopedia and answer the following questions.

5. Why is Sir Edmund Hillary famous? _____

6. What country was he from? _____

7. How did Hillary originally earn his living? _____

8. How high is Mount Everest? _____

DIRECTIONS Read the entry for *Zimbabwe* in an encyclopedia and answer the following questions.

9. Where is Zimbabwe located? _____

10. Does it have a coast? _____

11. What is the former name of Zimbabwe? _____

12. What are the most important agricultural products? _____

DIRECTIONS Read the entry for *rice* in an encyclopedia and answer the following questions.

13. Why is rice an important food crop? _____

14. Where is 90% of the world's rice grown? _____

15. How is most rice grown in Asia? _____

16. Where is the most rice eaten? _____

Using an Atlas

An **atlas** is a book of maps. The maps, charts, and text report the size, population, climate, rainfall, and natural resources of a region. A **map legend** shows what the symbols on the map represent. A **compass rose** tells where north, south, east, and west are on the map. Some compass roses include the intermediate directions (NW, SW, NE, SE).

DIRECTIONS ▷ Use an atlas of the United States to answer these questions about Tennessee.

1. What is the capital of Tennessee? _____

2. How many states border Tennessee? _____

   Which state lies on Tennessee's eastern border? _____

3. How many people live in Tennessee? _____

4. What national park is in Tennessee? _____

5. What interstate highway crosses the state from east to west? _____

6. In which direction would you travel from Knoxville to Nashville? _____

7. What mountain range is in Tennessee? _____

8. About how much money does each household in Tennessee earn per year? _____

DIRECTIONS ▷ Use a world atlas to answer these questions about Switzerland.

9. In what part of Europe is Switzerland located? _____

10. Is the country inland? _____ If not, which body of water borders it? _____

11. Name the countries that border Switzerland. _____

12. Which rivers run through Switzerland? _____

13. What is the capital of Switzerland? _____

14. What mountain range is in Switzerland? _____

15. What kind of climate does Switzerland have? _____

16. What languages do the people in Switzerland speak? _____

Using an Almanac

An **almanac** is a reference book that is published yearly. Almanacs give information on many topics of interest, such as weather forecasts, tides, times of sunrises, and astronomy information. Often the information in almanacs is provided in tables, graphs, and statistics.

Almanacs also contain articles on people who have made news during the past year. As an extra feature, almanacs often include lists of noteworthy people and events over a period of time. The subject matter of the lists varies from year to year.

DIRECTIONS ▷ **Use the information below from an almanac to answer the questions.**

Noted Aviators Through the Ages

Leonardo da Vinci	Italy 1452–1519
Jean P. Blanchard	France 1753–1809
the Montgolfier brothers	France 1740–1810
Salomon A. Andrée	Sweden 1854–1897
the Wright brothers	United States 1867–1948
Louis Blériot	France 1872–1936
Blanche S. Scott	United States 1892–1970
Amelia Earhart	United States 1897–1937 (?)
Charles A. Lindbergh	United States 1902–1974
Jacqueline Cochran	United States 1910–1980

1. Which noted aviator lived before the 1700s? _____

2. Which two countries have the greatest number of aviators listed? _____
_____

3. Which noted aviators lived into the twentieth century? _____
_____

4. Which noted aviators lived in only one century? _____
_____

5. According to this almanac, which country dominated aviation during the twentieth century?
_____

6. Which countries are represented only once in this list? _____

7. Which aviator's year of death is not known for certain? _____

Using References to Find Information

atlas—a book of maps
thesaurus—a book of synonyms and antonyms
dictionary—a book that gives the pronunciation and definitions of words
almanac—a book that is published each year and gives facts about various topics such as the tides, weather, time the sun rises, etc. Much of the information is presented in charts, tables, and graphs. An almanac also presents general information.
encyclopedia—a set of volumes that has articles about various topics
Books in Print—a book that lists books that have been published about various subjects

DIRECTIONS ▷ Write the correct reference source for each item of information. Choose from the list below. There may be more than one correct answer.

atlas	almanac	thesaurus	encyclopedia	dictionary	*Books in Print*	**WORD BOX**

1. **Languages** — It is estimated that there are thousands of languages spoken in the world. Following is a list of the major languages spoken by the greatest number of people. They are ranked in order of usage.

Name of Language	Major Areas Where Spoken
Chinese (Mandarin)	China
English (has the most words – 790,000)	U.S., U.K., Canada, Ireland, Australia, New Zealand

   _____

2. **sincere** — honest, truthful, honorable, frank, open, aboveboard, unreserved, veracious, true, candid

   _____

3. **writing** — visible recording of language peculiar to the human species. Writing permits the transmission of ideas over vast distances of time and space and is essential to complex civilization. The first known writing dates from 6000 B.C.

   _____

4. **language** [lang´ gwij] *n.* **1. a.** Spoken or written human speech. *Language* is used to communicate thoughts and feelings. **b.** A particular system of human speech that is shared by the people of a country or another group of people. **2.** Any system of signs, symbols, or gestures used for giving information.

   _____

5. books about soccer

   _____

The Dewey Decimal System

The **Dewey Decimal System** was published by Melvil Dewey in 1876 and is still used in most school libraries today. The DDS is a way to classify **nonfiction** books by dividing them into ten broad categories. The categories are organized as follows:

000–099	General reference books	500–599	Pure sciences
100–199	Philosophy	600–699	Technology
200–299	Religion	700–799	Arts and recreation
300–399	Social sciences	800–899	Literature
400–499	Linguistics/language	900–999	General geography and history

DIRECTIONS Answer the questions using the Dewey Decimal System chart above.

1. Michael needs to find the words to some popular rock songs. In which section will he probably find books of lyrics? _____

2. Where should Erica look for information about the religions of India? _____

3. Mario is doing a report on the differences in the pronunciation of Spanish in Puerto Rico, Cuba, and Mexico City. Where should he look? _____

4. Hoda wants to find out why certain speakers have better sound than others. Which section will probably have the information she needs? _____

5. Jasmine needs a copy of *The Historical Atlas of the 20th Century* to find information about the break-up of the British Empire. Where will she find the atlas? _____

6. Thieu wants to find a copy of Gary Paulsen's *Hatchet*. Which section contains the information he wants? _____

DIRECTIONS Write book titles or make up imaginary book titles that would be found under each of the following DDS classifications.

7. 300–399: _____

8. 500–599: _____

9. 700–799: _____

10. 900–999: _____

Using a Computerized Card Catalog

Libraries used to keep track of their inventory by having cards for each book. These cards were alphabetized and kept in "card catalogs." Most libraries now use **computerized card catalogs**. You can look up books by title, author, or subject. The computer can tell you whether the book is available or has been checked out. In public libraries in cities, you can find out which branches have the book if your location doesn't have it. Sometimes you can call another branch and have the book sent to the library closest to you.

DIRECTIONS ▷ **Refer to the directions inside the box to answer the questions.**

To look for a book by the author's last name:		To look for a book by title:	
STEP	**ACTION**	**STEP**	**ACTION**
1	Type: FA	1	Type: FT
2	Type: Author's last name	2	Type: Book title
3	Press: <RETURN> key	3	Press: <RETURN> key

1. Write the three steps you would follow to find a book by Thor Heyerdahl.

_____

_____

_____

2. Write the three steps you would take to find a book titled *Treasures of the Deep*.

_____

_____

_____

3. If you type FA to find a book by author's name, and you type FT to find a book by book title, what do you think you would type to find a book by subject? Explain your answer.

_____

_____

4. What three steps would you take to find books about whales?

_____

_____

_____

Computerized Card Catalog

Using the Internet for Research

You can use a computer to help you do research on the Internet. The World Wide Web allows you to access many websites that have pictures and sounds as well as written information. **Search engines** are instruments that help you find the information you want.

◎ ◎◎ ◎◎ ◎◎◎◎◎◎◎◎ ◎ ◎◎◎ ◎◎ ◎◎◎◎◎◎◎◎ ◎◎◎ ◎◎◎◎◎◎ ◎

DIRECTIONS ▷ Connect to the Internet. Use the search engine <u>www.yahooligans.com</u> to search for the subject *elephant*. Then, answer the questions.

1. How many category matches were listed? _____

2. How many site matches were listed? _____

3. Under which category do you find the most resources listed? _____

4. List the website addresses that have pictures of elephants. _____

_____

5. List the website addresses that have magazine articles listed. _____

_____

_____

DIRECTIONS ▷ Use these different search engines to do a search for the subject *elephant*. Then, answer the questions.

<u>www.yahooligans.com</u>	<u>www.ajkids.com</u>	<u>www.altavista.com</u>	**WORD BOX**

6. Which search engine gave you the best results? _____

7. Which search engine gave you the most results? _____

8. Which search engine was the easiest to use? _____

_____

9. Pick a topic that interests you and search the Internet for information. Which search engine(s) did you use? Tell what you found out about your topic. _____

_____

_____

_____

_____

Online Reference Materials

Many websites are available to help you find traditional reference resources. Many associations and organizations, such as the American Library Association, NASA, and the U.S. Library of Congress, have put their information online so that it is easy to access. The media specialist at your school or library can help you with both online and conventional methods of resource gathering.

DIRECTIONS ▷ **Use the websites listed below to answer the questions.**

Organization	Website
U.S. Library of Congress	http://lcweb.loc.gov/
The American Library Association	http://www.ala.org/ICONN/kcfavorites.html
The WWW Virtual Library	http://vlib.org/Overview.html
The Internet Public Library Youth Division	http://www.ipl.org/youth/

1. Which website contains information about the Dewey Decimal System? _____

2. Which websites have subjects listed alphabetically? _____

3. Which websites have subjects listed by categories? _____

4. Which is your favorite website? _____

5. Which website has a story hour section? _____

6. Which websites have fun activities for students to do? _____

7. Which websites do you think could help you the most on a research project? _____

8. Pick a subject that interests you. Use three different websites to find out more about the subject. List the three websites you used. Use your research to write a short description about the subject you chose. _____

Using Text Divisions and Emphasis

When you are reading for specific information, you will succeed more easily if you learn to use text divisions and emphasis tools. Important words often appear in **boldface** type, *italics*, or CAPS. **Subheads** and **marginal labels** help readers understand how the information is organized. They also help readers locate information more quickly.

DIRECTIONS ▸ **Answer the questions.**

1. In a science textbook, which word in the following paragraph might you expect to find in boldface print or italics? Why?

   Ice in the form of glaciers can change the shape of the land. Glaciers are large sheets of ice. As they move across the land, they pick up rocks and soil. Glaciers can carve valleys into the land and make hills level.

   _____

2. In a science textbook, under which of the following subheadings would you most likely find information about how waves change the shape of the land?

   Ice Changes Land
   Waves
   From Rain to Rivers

   _____

3. Write the question answered by these sentences from a social studies textbook.

   One reason Cuban Americans have been successful is their tradition of helping each other. For example, some of the first Cubans who came to the United States were wealthy professionals who were able to start their own businesses. These businesspeople gave many jobs to the Cubans who came later.

   _____

4. In a science textbook, which words in the following paragraph might you expect to find in boldface print or italics? Why?

   In the human body the circulatory system serves as a delivery system. The blood vessels are like canals carrying supplies everywhere. Some blood vessels are large and some are very small. They carry nutrients to every part of the body.

   _____

Adjusting Reading Rates

Students use different reading strategies depending on the type of material they are reading and their purpose for reading it. Readers use a **relaxed rate** when reading for pleasure. **Skimming** means looking over a book or reference source quickly to identify its subject and find out how it is organized. **Scanning** means looking quickly through a passage to find key words or phrases. Scanning is a fast way to locate specific information.

DIRECTIONS Read the selections and answer the questions.

porcine [pôr sin] *adj.* of, relating to, or suggesting swine, pigs, or hogs.

Amanda was not expecting a pig as a pet. A cat, a dog, even a gerbil would have seemed better suited to her family's suburban home. The pig had turned up unannounced, unsolicited, and unfed at her very doorstep. No one knew where it came from or to whom it belonged. It was a homeless pig. There were already too many "uns" in this pig's life. Amanda wasn't going to let it be unloved as well.

HOG A mature specimen of the family Suidae, raised extensively in most areas of the world for food. These cloven-hoofed animals have round bodies and short legs and are also referred to as pigs or swine. Domestic breeds include the Chester White, Berkshire, Spotted Poland, Chine, and Yorkshire.

1. How would you read a piece to skim for information? _____

_____

2. How would you read a piece to scan for information? _____

_____

3. Which of these selections would you scan? _____

_____

4. Which selection might you read at a relaxed rate? _____

_____

5. How would you read the dictionary entry to prepare for a vocabulary test? _____

_____

6. Which selection might you read slowly, taking notes as you read? Why might you do this?

_____

_____

Taking Notes

Taking notes helps you organize information when you do research. Some facts are more important than others. Write down only the main ideas when you take notes.

DIRECTIONS ▷ **Read the following paragraphs and take notes about them on the note cards below.**

Among women in history, Queen Hatshepsut of Egypt holds a special place. She was the only woman ever to rule Egypt with the all-powerful title of pharaoh. Hatshepsut succeeded her husband Thutmose II to the throne about 1504 B.C. She enjoyed a relatively long reign, ruling as pharaoh for twenty-one years. During that time, Hatshepsut was remarkably productive. Egypt's trade improved under her leadership, and she embarked on a major building program.

NOTES
_____
_____
_____
_____
_____
_____

Meng T'ien, the general in charge of building the Great Wall, is also credited with another, smaller construction project. Sometime before 200 B.C., General T'ien is believed to have invented the *cheng*, a musical instrument of the zither family. Like other zithers of Asia, the *cheng* has a long, slightly curved sound box with strings that stretch the length of the instrument. Frets, or stops, are located on the sound box to help produce the melody. Although the *cheng* is no longer popular in China, its descendants are still popular in other Asian countries. In Vietnam, the *tranh* is still used for courtly music, and the *koto* enjoys wide popularity in Japan.

NOTES
_____
_____
_____
_____
_____
_____

Outlines

An **outline** organizes information into main topics, subtopics, and details. An outline follows certain rules of capitalization and punctuation.

DIRECTIONS Write *main topic*, *subtopic*, or *detail* to identify each item in this part of an outline.

I. Loch Ness monster _____

   A. Where it lives _____

      1. Northern Scotland _____

      2. Deep, narrow lake _____

   B. What it looks like _____

      1. Small head _____

      2. Long, thin neck _____

      3. Body 90 feet long _____

DIRECTIONS The information in this outline is in the correct order. Find the error or errors in each line, and write the line correctly. Remember to indent the lines properly.

II. the Yeti _____

   a. where it lives _____

      1. in Asia _____

      2. in the Himalayas _____

   b. what it looks like _____

      1. large ape or man _____

      2. covered with hair _____

DIRECTIONS Research famous monsters or other imaginary creatures. Write an outline of the information you find. Revise and proofread your work, checking for correct outline form.